G. B

THE MAN IN THE STREET

DAVID MARSHALL

THE MAN
IN THE STREET

DAVIS-POYNTER
London

First published in 1976 by
Davis-Poynter Limited
20 Garrick Street London WC2E 9BJ

Copyright ©1976 by David Marshall

ISBN 0 7067 0209 3

Photoset by Red Lion Setters
Holborn, London
Printed in Great Britain by
A Wheaton & Co
Hennock Rd
Exeter
EX2 8RP

To the dustmen of Barnsley

Acknowledgements

My profound thanks to my family, to Mr and Mrs Peter Hunt and to Mr Frank Parkinson for their criticisms and observations, and to Mrs Doris Lowes for producing the typescript.

Contents

Acknowledgements	*page*	6
Glossary		8
Preface		9
1 The Interview		11
2 Initiation		18
3 The Cardboard Lorry		32
4 Pogmoor		45
5 The Cleanest Road		66
6 Binning		80
7 Further Education		91
8 The Spare Wagon		101
9 Sparky		112
10 The House		123
11 Last Days		134

Glossary

In Yorkshire dialect the word 'the' is often reduced to 't'', but more often than not it is only apparent as a brief pause in a person's speech. I have represented this pause by a single apostrophe, thus 'into the yard' reads 'into ' yard'.

allus	always
an' all	as well; too
bahn	going
baht	without
fast on	asleep
flog	sell
fun	found
gied	given
'afe	half
lace	beat soundly
laik	i) be ill; ii) play
na	than
neet	night
noddle	head
pem	stink
reight	i) extremely; ii) right
skive	abscond

Preface

The Man In The Street can fairly be described as a dustman's diary. The events took place during the summers of 1969 and 1970 in the Yorkshire town of Barnsley — not Barnsley as it is today, rearing a brood of uncompromising concrete and glass complexes amongst spacious precincts and dual-carriageways, but the old town with its fancy, almost smug, architecture that so typified nineteenth-century prosperity, its open markets and its intricate web of narrow streets and tiny passageways. And it did all happen: the incidents are true and the people involved were real dustmen; only their names have been changed. The result may not be a flattering portrayal of dustmen, but who would volunteer to become a better example? After all, they did not pretend about themselves, so it seems only proper to reciprocate by having no illusions about them either. It was Lampy the road-sweeper who put their position in its proper perspective, one hot summer's day in 1970, as he explained why his union was demanding an immediate wage increase, and the force of his honesty was exposed to the nation in the following October, when the country's dustmen and sewage workers went on strike.

'' way Ah see it is this. Tha can look at ' country just like a 'uman body, an' everyone i' ' country is a part on it, like. So tha can say as ' government is its brain, an' where we 'ave feet, ' country 'as railways. We all 'ave summat to do, an' even if some on us is more important na others we all depend on each other, choose if tha're ' most important or ' least. Now us dustmen are only ' arse-end, an' tha gets these folk who look down on thee for it. But it's a daft attitude, that, 'cos thi arse is as important as owt else tha's got an' should be treated wi' respect. Like Ah say, if tha don't pay proper attention to it, it starts to itch ... an' tha knows thissen, when thi arse itches, tha're forced to scratch it.'

1 The Interview

No-one had ever told me how difficult it was to become a dustman. At that time, I laboured under a fairly common misunderstanding that there must be a severe shortage of them as the dustbins never seemed to be emptied regularly and the streets were invariably adorned with litter. Besides, it is not a career which immediately brings to mind the sort of glamour and excitement that might draw you to become, say, an airline pilot, or a British secret agent, or a king, so that, far from having to compete with scores of eager applicants it seemed that if you could only find your way into the appropriate office the job was yours on demand. There was probably no need to go equipped with certificates and references either: provided you could fit a lid on a dustbin or hold a roadsweeper's brush in both hands without falling over they could not afford to refuse you.

Matters were not quite so simple, however, as I discovered that particular summer when I returned from university to Barnsley with four months' holiday in front of me, and decided to fill in some of that time working in local government. There was good reason for choosing to be a dustman. Amongst my fellow students it was a well known fact that escorting a rubbish cart around town could be very lucrative vacation work and the pickings were ripe. To a poverty-stricken undergraduate dreaming of a fortnight's holiday basking on foreign shores, earning the fare by walking about for a few weeks with a dustbin attached to one's shoulder seemed like getting money for old rope. Besides, even this mild inconvenience was now a thing of the primitive past. 'It's all done up in paper bags now,' said someone who had come to this enviable arrangement with a neighbouring local authority in the previous long-vacation. 'And you've only to lift fifty a day. You'll knock two hundred quid up in ten weeks easily.'

The sound of 200 voices in full flood was ringing in my ears as I alighted from the bus in Barnsley. I had decided not to repeat an earlier mistake of writing off for the job. It appeared to be a settled fact of life within the Cleansing Department that anyone who wrote requesting an application form for the post of temporary road-sweeper could not seriously be wanting work. The most effective approach in this case was to avoid polite formality and to seek a down-to-earth confrontation. This way the matter could be settled without delay: either I got the job or was told that they could only deal with me by letter.

The Departmental offices were situated, according to the telephone directory, along Pontefract Road. Somehow, I failed to notice them and was well on the way to Pontefract when this chilling truth dawned. Tired and confused, I retraced my steps. Someone at the glass works had last seen them lurking around the next corner. So I followed his directions and, coming upon a drive, proceeded down it towards a close family of buildings. Under the nearest porch someone seemed to have planted a lamp-post in a pair of boots but, as I approched, it quickly sprouted arms and legs and there, in its place, was an extremely thin man rescued from invisibility by his white coat, trousers and a pair of spectacles.

'Is this the Cleansing Department?' I inquired.

The man looked round at me. His head was little more than a skull and it reflected something of my own horror.

'Do I look like a dustman?'

In all honesty he did not, but he could well have been something that had fallen off the refuse lorry.

'This is Oakwell Brewery. What do you want?'

'I'm job hunting.'

'Never heard of you! What are you doing down here?'

'I'm looking for the Cleansing Department.'

'Ah! Well! It's not here. This is Oakwell Brewery.'

'I came down here thinking it was the Cleansing Department.'

'Can't imagine why. What do you want to go there for?'

'I'm looking for a job.'

'Sorry! Can't help you. This is Oakwell Brewery. We don't have jobs here. What do you want a job for?'

'It's not the job I want. It's the money.'

'Student, eh? Thought so. Living off the taxpayers and still not satisfied. Well, we don't take students on. Lazy sods, students. Ought to be in the army, the lot of you.'

'Actually, I hadn't come for a job here.'

'See what I mean? Typical! All play and no work makes Jack a student. Don't know what the country's coming to. To think we fought the last war for such as you.'

'I meant I didn't know there were no jobs available at this place.'

'Now steady on! Never said that. Matter of fact we are a bit under-staffed at present. We could do with a couple of driver's mates — you know, delivering to the pubs and that.'

'In fact, what I was really thinking of doing was ...'

'No! It's no good you asking. You couldn't do it. Too skinny. Rolling full barrels on and off lorries needs a real man, someone with a bit of meat on him.'

Within the deep folds of his coat, his pencil-thin body seemed to swell slightly.

'In that case, perhaps I'd better try the Cleansing Department.'

'Good idea! And if you have no luck there, there's just a chance you might get on here. We've a store man leaving shortly and you could probably just about do his job. Think about it!'

Back once more on Pontefract Road I continued the search, but without success. It was somewhere in the vicinity, but where? On the hillside to the left lay the abbatoir, and below me a large, old house built of stone reclined in the shade of a thick belt of tall trees. There was nothing that looked remotely likely to contain dustmen. Perhaps secrecy in its whereabouts was deliberate departmental policy: certainly, it would not then have to deal with many complaints.

There was a drive curling through the wood and it seemed as reasonable to take its course as any. The path led past the old stone house, which turned out to be Beevor Hall, and headed in the direction of certain, more modern buildings which seemed depressingly familiar. Before I could beat a quick retreat, the man in the white coat stepped out of the hall.

'You back again! I didn't mean he was going that soon. No, give it a week or two and we'll contact you. Better still, write to us and then we've got you on the file.'

I fled.

Eventually, and at no small cost to my shoes, I came upon the

Department's lair. It was cunningly concealed for the most part behind a row of terraced houses that dressed themselves from the junction of Pontefract Road with Langdale Road. This setting presented to passers-by just a few single-storey buildings and the entrance to an empty yard. A dull-red paint coated the woodwork, and it was modestly identified in small letters on the gate. The whole melted into the background as if it were ashamed of its associatons. Anyone could have missed it: I had.

'We normally only deal with this sort of thing by letter,' said a typist who was solid paint from the neck to her peroxide crown and was in the process of applying a second coat. 'Would you like to write in?'

I declined the pleasure. She continued to work mascara into her eyeballs.

'It's most inconvenient, you see. The Superintendent is very busy right now.'

With the aid of a mirror she rouged her cheeks with all the skill of an undertaker and to much the same effect. Evidently, her superior's disease was not catching. Her face was being trans-formed before my very eyes. It was almost lunch time and this creation was clearly the one she went out in; it was weather-proof and vinyl-finished.

'I can wait.'

She sighed. She could not. Her face now bloomed with all the natural vigour of a neon-lit advertisement and she was desperate to display her applied charms before corrosion set in.

'I'll ask him if he'll see you,' she said, graciously, as she swirled out of the room.

A few moments later her poker face reappeared round the door.

'You can go in now. But he can't spare a lot of time. And don't say I didn't warn you.'

The immediate prospect of an audience so grudgingly granted found me nervous and trembling, and I stepped into the sanctuary of the awesome personage almost on tiptoe. The office was, belying the hazards of getting into it, hardly palatial. Strewn across the shelves on the far wall were a half-dozen or so well-worn files that looked as though they had been salvaged from one of the rounds. The walls were that delicate shade of brown which more than suggested that they were originally cream. In the middle, surrounded by what apologized for being a carpet, was an old, wooden, ink-stained desk and sitting behind it was the Superintendent. He was busily drinking a cup of very strong-smelling coffee and reading a newspaper. My entrance did not for a moment disturb his concentration. In fact for a full two minutes he managed, in a very grand manner, to ignore me, while he perused the cricket reports on the back page. As the seconds ticked by I could feel my self-confidence, already much abated, leaking rapidly out of my shoes. I stood just inside the door and tried to look equally indifferent by watching a fly crawling up the side of a window. When I checked to see what effect this was having on the Superintendent, he was watching the fly too. In despair, I coughed. Rather half-heartedly he stopped staring at the window and turned to see what was making all the noise. He did not seem altogether impressed.

'Sit down!'

Was it an order or an invitation? I sat down. Fortunately, there was a chair behind me.

'So you've come for a job, young man?'

I squeaked affirmatively. Or was it the chair? There was a clock muttering inanely somewhere in the background; it seemed to be sniggering at me.

'You're a student?' he said in tones implying a sin in the condition.

I confessed at once.

'We do take students on, sometimes — only during the holidays, of course. But it's no use me setting you on unless you're suitable: we've scores of students asking for work and we can only take the best. We've found in past years, that some of you have not been quite up to it. College boys come here who haven't even the strength to brush their own hair, let alone the streets. So if there's anything wrong with you ...'

He paused. I followed his example.

'Well?'

'Yes, thank you.'

Clearly, he was not convinced. I could feel his gaze searching my jacket for odd lumps that betrayed artificial limbs, calipers and external heart resuscitators. He seemed disappointed by their absence.

'No asthma?' he asked, desperately. 'Or flat feet?'

I shook my head.

'Epilepsy?'

Another shake.

'Paralysis of some sort, then? It's common enough in workmen.'

I was going dizzy with effort.

'Well, if we take you on, you realize you can be called on to do any number of jobs. You might be told to sweep streets or work a few days on the tip or spray weeds with caustics. And you'll probably have to work on the dustbin rounds at some time. Now that is hard work. One dustbin weighs about sixty pounds. Can you really lift a hundred of those in a day?'

Scorn fairly dribbled from his last words. And yet it was an outrageously pointless question. It was like asking if I could balance peas on a knife-blade whilst standing on my head in a canoe ploughing through eighty-foot-high waves. I did not know because I had never tried.

'Yes!' I said.

Later I was to discover that the bluff was by no means one-sided. Anyone who believes that any dustbin with the borough of Barnsley could, with seven days' accumulated rubbish in it, weigh as little as sixty pounds either never struggled beyond his four-times table or is a pitiful martyr to monstrous illusions.

'Well, in that case,' he relented, with some hesitation, 'We'll see what you can do. When can you start?'

I opened my mouth — a habit of mine when speaking.

'Next Monday, then,' he continued. 'The hours are seven o'clock till four, and you've twenty minutes for breakfast, twelve till one for lunch. Clock-in outside the inspector's office. Any questions?'

From the tone of his voice, I deduced that there were no questions. It was all settled and I made ready to leave.

'Just one more thing, young man,' he added.

My senses lurched. You know full well when someone casually throws out that line that he is about to drop a bombshell in its wake.

'You are over twenty-one aren't you?'

'Twenty.'

'In that case you won't be paid at the full rate. The wages here range from between thirteen to fourteen pounds depending on whether you are sweeping streets or emptying dustbins. But as you're not adult you only get ninety per cent of a man's wage. And since we have students doing the calculations in the Wages Office, you'd better check to see that you're getting even that.'

Only when I was once more on Pontefract Road did I consider briefly that the arrangement was only fair if I had to work just ninety per cent as hard as a regular. But that was not now the agreement. It was incredible that Barnsley Borough Council, socialist to the last button on its Co-operative suits, could contemplate equality in terms that if it employed child (or at least non-adult) labour, ten per cent of that, regardless of effort and individual merit, should be slave labour in all but name. At that precise moment, however, it was difficult, not to say tiresome, to pay attention to those subversive voices of resentment and frustration. The sun was shining, the birds were singing; laughter floated lightly on the breeze, and I was a dustman.

2 Initiation

The sky was a delicate blue, pale and wishy-washy as though God, caught short of paint that morning, had been hastily diluting it. Thin wisps of cloud stretched across the southern horizon like untidy patches of exposed canvas. I walked briskly down Wesley Street between high, dark-stained brick walls with their white-veiled windows staring vacantly at the intruder. It was just a quarter to seven and the earth was resting before the roaring armies of traffic from north, south, east and west clashed in a day long battle in Barnsley's busy centre. Even the air was still. The street was strewn with cigarette packets, sweet wrappings, and the red and green bingo cards smuggled out from the old Alhambra Picture Palace. 'Meet Friends, Make Friends' insisted the posters. Only a few hours ago thousands of footsteps would have chorused their reply: now the last remains of the night's courtship had fallen unheeded like the leaves of autumn. I surveyed the sorrowful aftermath with a new and not dispassionate interest. Some poor wretch of a road-sweeper had to clean up this mess. An acute sense of kinship evoked strong sympathies for the unwitting individual who was going to find himself sweeping Wesley Street that day, while at the same time I hoped that Fate would not be so unkind to me.

In time I became accustomed to the first stirrings of life in the terrace row overshadowing Pontefract Road as it wound its way beneath the railway bridge. Invariably, a man in his braces and shirt-sleeves would emerge from one of the middle houses and wrestle a scuttleful of coal from the dark recess of his coal shed. Two doors away and upstairs a woman sat by her dressing table combing out her long, fine hair (black on Mondays, Wednesdays and alternate Fridays). But as yet, the recurring patterns of this particular kaleidoscope were strange to me, movements interesting in themselves and lacking any useful interpretation. Thus the passage of the grumbling diesel train from Barnsley to Sheffield over Pontefract Road meant nothing that first time; later, I was to understand that if I failed to beat it to the bridge only a brisk trot, totally out of step with the philosophy of a public servant, would prevent the works' clock eating into my wages.

There were two purpose-built entrances to the premises of the Cleansing Department, a small gate for the office staff and, a few yards away, the main entry used by motor traffic, manual workers and the local dogs. By this latter opening stood the super-intendent's office like a permanent sentry, its tireless eye seemingly missing nothing. Beyond, several long buildings bordered on to a large yard; a storehouse, a repair shop, a place for bailing cloth remnants from the tailors. At the far end were the corrugated-iron garages for the electric dust-carts, while immediately in front of them, with one side open to the yard, was a shed containing the hand-barrows, one or two giant-size dustbins and about three-quarters of the labour-force. Hidden behind the garages was the canteen — strategically situated near to the fish-and-chip shop in Langdale Road — where the lunch time activities would have brought pangs of homesickness to any holidaying croupier from Monte Carlo. And in the very centre of the yard, like a rusty island in a sea of gray asphalt, crouched a tiny, brick building that was conspicuous only by its solitude and which, despite its lowly size, was the inspector's office.

A constant stream of men was passing through a kind of porch attached to this modest hut intent on the serious business of 'clocking-on'. My card was one of the last to be stamped — '6.59 am'. Despite very kind instructions on it as to the correct way to insert it into the machine I persistently had it stamped on the blank, reverse side for the entire week. The Wages Clerk was in no way troubled by the resultant gibberish.

'Student?' he asked; and a nod was a sufficient explanation.

'Don't leave it too late, nip,' said a regular called Charlie who took an early interest in my career. 'If tha're ovver three minutes late, they knock thi quarter of an hour off thi wages.'

'I suppose that's fair.'

'Don't talk daft! They work it all i' their favour. More often than not Ah'm 'ere twenty minutes early — on account o' ' buses

— an' they've nivver paid me a penny ovvertime. By Gow, Ah'd be up 'ere at five if they did.'

The appointed hour had come, but there was nothing about the peaceful atmosphere in the yard to indicate the fact with any confidence. Perhaps fifty or so workmen slouched idly around in groups discussing the day's racing certainties or Saturday's punting upsets, the bargain-buy in the market and the increase in rents. Naive-looking youths in jeans and old school blazers intermingled with them, relishing in the calculation of odds some practical use for an A-level in mathematics.

'Students,' Charlie confided, as though the fact were not obvious.

The only person who appeared in any sense active was someone with a singularly long neck who from time to time would lean out of the open door of the inspector's office and peer round the yard, jerking his head from one position to the other like a hen pecking grain. He was Stan, the yard foreman, so Charlie said, a kind of quartermaster-cum-steward whose official responsibilities were to supervise the stocks, issue equipment to the men and generally keep the yard in order. In fact he had been there for so long and knew the workings of the depot so thoroughly that a succession of inspectors had come to rely on him as a deputy who would sort out the problems they could not understand. But although he was the ablest of lieutenants, he was terrified at the prospect of having to assume charge of operations should the inspector fail to turn up one morning. So, Charlie explained, if the inspector had not arrived by seven, Stan would begin an increasingly nervous look-out and if there was still no sign of him by quarter-past you could guarantee the foreman would be vomiting into a bucket.

At a few minutes after seven o'clock a small, dark-red van with the corporation crest half-mutilated on its dusty flanks swept through the entrance and managed to halt itself fractionally before invoking the aid of the office wall. Cries of 'Begorra' and 'It's the Shamrock Kid' greeted the driver. Michael O'Grady was the inspector in charge and it was always his arrival that signalled the beginning of the working day. Stan stumbled out of the office wiping the perspiration off his forehead, and all but a few men left their cosy perches to amble over in Mike's direction, rather like a herd of Friesians at milking time.

'Tha's just come reight, nip,' Charlie revealed. 'We'd a i'spector not long sin' as nivver let thi alone. Allus checkin' up on us an' tellin' ' tale to ' boss if we did owt wrong. We were fair glad when 'e got promoted. But Mike's all reight; 'e's one of us.'

The lorries thundered into the yard. The Cleansing Department hired all its vehicles and drivers from the Highways Department, although the functions, additional to the obvious one, to which a refuse lorry could be put so as to make this arrangement practical were never made known. Most of them were modern, silver-sided monsters with grimy, cavernous mouths gaping from their backs, but there was also one of the old semi-cylindrical side-loaders and a sparse assortment of covered vans and low-sided tipping lorries — no more than a score of vehicles all told. As they entered, their respective crews hobbled towards them, were counted and swallowed.

'We're one short, Mike! Ben's missin'.'

'Take Roy, then. But look after him 'cos he's only little. And make sure he doesn't get sucked in with the rubbish.'

'Carlton need an extra man, Mike.'

'Let me go wi' 'em, Mike!'

'Now, how can I let you go binning, mi old son. You've got them sloping shoulders: You'd have a bin empty before you got to the lorry. No, you go, Johnny. And if there's a pair of gloves in the cab, wear them. We don't want you dirtying our dustbins.'

'Am Ah weed sprayin' again?'

'I don't know yet. We've been having complaints from the weeds. They say you're killing them. Let me deal with the binners first. Archie! ... Archie! God! Where's he left his ears this morning? ARCHIE! You've to make sure you empty that shop on Lindhurst Road. He told me last week you took the bin and left the rubbish.'

'Ahh! Well! It weren't our fault. ' bottom fell aht as we picked it up. An' it were packed that solid it just sat there lookin' like one o' our lass's fruit cakes.'

'Well, in that case you could do her a favour and buy her a cookery book. Oh, and before you go, warn Cyril not to smoke his pipe when he's driving. The fire brigade were chasing him on Friday.'

So the orders of the day were distributed. Words tumbled from his lips in brilliant profusion: he did not speak them; his brogue chuckled mischievously over them. Sarcasm, wit, wisecracks came as naturally to him as walking comes to a millepede. Seemingly as an incidental by-product, he also performed his duties. One by one, the lorries roared out their warcries and dispersed to the various fronts in the borough. Next, he turned to the road-sweepers, checking each unit off his chart.

'Good Heavens, Billy! What have you done to your brush? I've seen bigger bristles on toothbrushes.'

'It's worn aht, Mike.'

'Worn out?! You only signed out for it two weeks ago. You must be shaving it. Or did it go bald with the shock of you actually using it?'

'A man can't do his job baht good tools.'

'The rate you're going through them, we shan't even have bad ones. Get him another, Stan, steel tipped if possible; we'll have to measure his bristles every night now till we get to the bottom of this. And how's Charlie?'

'Ah'm all reight.'

' "Charlie's all right", he says. That's what we want to hear. We could do with more Charlies in this place, couldn't we Stan?'

The last barrow rolled tragically out of the corner, its driver far too committed to his thoughts to be concerned with the perils on the road in front of him. Peace fell easily on the yard again. But apart from me there were only two people to appreciate it this time; the inspector and someone calling himself Tug Spooner, a sad looking man in his thirties who, I had discovered only moments before, was also making his debut that day.

'Have I forgotten you, lads?' Mike inquired, when he turned round and noticed us. 'You're both new, aren't you?'

'Yes.'

'Well, there's not a lot left for you. There's only that barrow' — he pointed to a yellow hand-cart lying in the shadow of a dustbin under the shed — 'Do you think you can handle a couple of brushes in the street without becoming a public menace?'

'Where shall we go?'

Stan, who was now happily at work in the office, pushed his head out of the window.

'New Street, Wellington Street, Pitt Street and Princess Street.'

'There you are. Settled now! You can see yourselves out, can't you? And whoever pushes the cart, remember there's a thirty-mile-an-hour speed limit.'

'What shall we do when we've finished those roads?'

Mike looked at Stan in disbelief. Stan clutched the window ledge to prevent himself swooning to the ground. They both began to laugh.

'You really are new,' observed Mike.

He disappeared into the office, still laughing.

Tug pushed his thumbs into his overall pockets and scowled at the little barrow under the shed.

'Ah'm not pushin' that: it's degradin'.'

'One of us has got to. We can't be walking a mile back here every time we have a shovelful of dirt.'

'Arr! One of us 'as to; but Ah'm not doin' it.'

By common consent, therefore, it was I who pushed the Corporation's No 11 barrow up the incline towards the town centre. Being made of fibre-glass it was not a heavy burden, but being empty, headstrong and in the hands of inexperience it caused havoc to traffic attempting to overtake it. My work-mate accompanied us slightly in advance and keeping well over to the far side of the footpath. The few people who passed us he would stare fiercely out of countenance and his hands would thrust stubbornly deeper into his pockets. He was slightly taller than me, with a magnificant physique that made me feel pigeon-chested. His bull-neck was stretched high and his sandy hair flamed with pride, but his honest face could not disguise his embarrassment.

'If mi Dad was alive to see mi now, 'e'd die o' shame. Tha're better off bein' o' ' dole than i' this caper — at least folk can only look down on thee once a week when tha're queuein' up. Ah've a good mind to go into Boots when they open an' get a pair o' dark glasses: ' only trouble is, Ah'd still know who Ah were, an' if Ah wore a suit o' armour Ah'd still be a dustman ... Don't it worry thee?'

'No! Besides, I can't afford the sun-glasses.'

'It's different for thee. Tha considered thissen a student even though tha're doin' ' same job as me. Me; Ah'm nowt more than what folk see me as — a road-sweeper; scum.

'Ah should nivver 'ave come 'ere if Ah 'adn't lost mi job. Ah

used to be in cement — workin' i' ' kilns. It were 'ard graft, but '
brass were worth it — tha could make thirty pound easy wi' a bit o'
ovvertime. Ah were doin' nicely; just bought mi Mam a telly an' a
washin' machine, an' on ' day Ah put down ' deposit for a bike,
they said they'd 'ave to sake mi — redundancy, tha sees. Well,
thirty-six is a poor age to be laid off. Tha're too young to retire an'
too old to start learnin' a new trade. Ah'm no use to anyone, tha
sees, baht a skill i' mi 'ands. Ah reckon that's 'ow 'afe these
men come to be doin' this job. Someone throws thee on ' muck'eap
an' tells thee to start shiftin' it. It don't make sense. It's same work
as Ah were doin' — only dirtier — tha gets less pay by 'afe an'
folks spit i' thi face.'

'I haven't seen much spittle flying around.'

'Tha knows what Ah mean.'

Stopping at the bottom of New Street, we made a reconnaissance
of the area. The town had been blitzed on the previous Saturday
with one of the heaviest and most violent cloud-bursts in living
memory. Clouds often weep over the sooty, perspiring face of
Barnsley and occasionally are so grieved by a man's mutilations of
it that their tears all but wash his sins away. To speak of 'The
Flood' in Barnsley is not always a reference to the Bible; you are
just as likely to be discussing the last heavy rain. That particular
Saturday had witnessed, within the space of twenty minutes, the
birth of a mighty river that swept irresistibly through the centre,
rearranging the siting arrangement of the market stalls, the market
customers and the traffic, pilfering wherever possible, and
performing remarkably unfair exchanges. Mike O'Grady later told
me that an old woman who had just bought her finnan haddock in
Kendray Street Market paid a traffic warden on her sudden
migration towards the 'bus station. Elsewhere a stallholder was left
with the pockets of his denim jackets and jeans stuffed with offal.
The deluge plundered the heart of the town and then raced for the
Dearne Valley, carrying along hundreds of pounds worth of goods,
some paid for and some not, shoppers' shoes, pet dogs, traffic
installations, furniture and sewage. When it comes to devastation
Nature has no equal.

New Street carves its path on the hillside, and as the waters had
rushed along they had poured in through the shop doorways and
carpeted the floors with a fine silt. The shopkeepers had quickly

brushed it out again, and now generous heaps of drying mud were lying in the gutters. The impression they gave us was that there were too many shops in New Street.

'Look on the bright side. At least we've only to shovel and not sweep.'

A light breeze playfully scattered the pyramids' outer coatings over the pavement. Armed with shovels we attacked the mounds of shop soil. Two girls in smocks hung over the counter, watching us and giggling.

'Just look at 'em! Laughin' 'cos they think we're too thick to mind.'

'Perhaps they fancy us?'

'Ahh! They do. They fancy we're t' silliest lookin' fools i' Barnsley. Ah wonder which one swept their shop aht this mornin.' Per'aps if we'd come earlier, we might 'ave 'ad a laugh.'

The bottom of New Street fairly radiated cleanliness before we turned off into Wellington Street. Tug did not sweep dust away: he fought it, bullied it, bludgeoned it into submission and then cast it exhausted on to the barrow: in his fiercer moments, it seemed he was even pulverizing the pavement. What he continually disregarded, however, was dog manure. At first, I thought this was due to some form of blindness, but it turned out that, in his philosophy, what was not good enough for a dog was not good enough for him.

There were no half-measures about Tug. Whatever he did was done with something approaching fanaticism. He left footpaths and gutters in a condition fit for surgeons to operate on them, and when we came upon long ribbons of green grass flourishing along the bottom of the church wall in Pitt Street, he went down on his hands and knees to pull them out, even going to the extent of ferreting the roots from the crevices in the wall with his penknife.

'Ah think a man should 'ave a pride in his work else there's no point i' doin' it. Mi old foreman used to 'ave us sweepin' aht by ' kiln floors till tha could see thi face in 'em. They were good days, them. But, like owt else, tha nivver knows 'ow good till it's gone.

'Ah'm gettin' wed this 'ere Christmas. That's why Ah were forced to take this job when Ah got ' sack. She's already got two young uns. Divorced like — 'e were a conductor for Tracky.* 'E

* Yorkshire Traction Co Ltd, which provided the town's public transport.

put 'er best mate i' ' club and then when 'e were bahn to marry 'er they found 'e'd just done t' same to a conductress, so 'e 'ad to scarper. 'E didn't mind when 'e found aht Ah were courtin' 'er — in fact, 'e wouldn't charge me mi fare. We'll live at Athersley where she is now, on ' estate. She'll not 'ave to go aht to work then, 'cos she's got asthma. We're puttin' mi Mam i' t' spare room so she can 'elp our lass when she gets an attack.

'Ah nivver thought Ah'd marry. Settlin' down meant a slow paralysis to me. In those days Ah were all for laikin' football an' a drink wi' t' lads. But she's best thing that's ever 'appened to me — tha'll know what Ah mean when it 'appens to thee. She's a good un, our Maureen, an' they're grand kids ... Ehee, she's a nice bit o'stuff, i'nt she?'

He nodded towards a tall, blonde figure tapping along the opposite side of the street on her high, stiletto heels.

''Ow are yer, love? All reight? (Tha's got to butter 'em up, tha sees.) It's turned aht nice for yer, 'a'nt it?'

She flashed a warm smile and made some flirting reply, but her pace never faltered. Unabashed, Tug watched her go, and then, turning round, perhaps imagined faint surprise in my expression.

'Not till Christmas,' he reminded me with a pregnant grin.

We finished weeding neatly on the stroke of twelve. It was lunch time, and there is nothing like pulling grass up from the base of church walls to give one an appetite. Neither of us had brought any food, but there was no shortage of snack-bars and pubs just down the hill. We stopped at a little café half way along Wellington Street and bought ourselves bacon sandwiches liberally spiced with brown sauce, which we ate while sitting on the kerb-stones with the warm sun branding a tan on our cheeks. From there we passed on to a pub, not only to quench a thirst brought on by the heat of the morning and bacon sandwiches, but also to while away the hour with an indoor game or two. Tug was at first reluctant to go in, being worse than rubbish at such things he said, which was why I insisted, and eventually he gave way. I have often wondered, since then, what bitter nuances he intended 'worse than rubbish' to imply. His difficulty in playing darts seemed to be an inability to hit anything but 'double-top', and when we turned to bar-billiards he won three games before I had even scored. Long before the end I was deeply sorry for having exposed this kind of weakness, especially against his will, and he was very quiet as we laid the cues in their resting hooks. At once he went over to the landlord standing behind the bar.

''As thi toilet got somewhere to wash mi 'ands in, mate?'

'Nay, old love. There's no demand. Folks aren't that posh in 'ere. They're glad enough just to be able to 'ave a piss i' private.'

'Well, can Ah use thi sink afore Ah go to ' toilet?'

The landlord stared at him stone-faced. The barmaid started to giggle.

'Where Ah come from, we were told to wash us 'ands after, lad. What's up? 'As tha got summat special?'

'Mi 'ands are mucky. Ah've been grassin' all mornin'.'

With the barmaid a few feet away, the landlord swore only very mildly and disappeared into the back room. Tug waited at the bar, his head hung low and his cheeks flaming scarlet. The other returned shortly and passed over to him a pair of sugar tongs.

'Ah'm fair sorry Ah've nowt to unfasten thi fly wi', but tha can manage wi' these.'

Everyone in the saloon fell about with laughing. The young barmaid collapsed on the counter and went into hysterics. Only Tug was unaffected by the gaiety. His eyes moistened and his colour deepened; he was a picture of painful misery. The landlord seemed even sterner than before.

'Don't tha want 'em then? Not big enough for thee, eh? Are tha fancyin' thissen i' front o' young lass? Will a pair o' coal tongs do?'

The afternoon sun was oppressively hot. We toiled along Princess Street, getting tacit sympathy from one or two faces sheltering within their cool, terraced houses, but sympathy casts little shade. Our coats, stuffed into a box between the two rubbish bins, were flecked with light-grey powder. The shovels seemed to be getting unbearably heavy and the cart increasingly more difficult to push. Worst of all was the depressing vision that afflicts the man labouring behind a long-handled brush that the road stretches twice as far as it actually does.

How thankful we were to be back in New Street, for at least the road was now downhill all the way. We worked steadily down towards our starting point, maintaining a lead of a few yards over an elderly couple out for an afternoon stroll. The man could walk only sloth-like and with the aid of a steel frame, while his wife relied on a stick. Their joy must have known no bounds to find that after a lifetime's faithful payment of the rates, the corporation had not forgotten them in their declining years but had sent two of its employees to clear the most trifling hazards from their path. It must have been worth a drop in pension.

Some time after three o'clock, we leaned our shovels against the barrow and ourselves against the fence, to take a welcome break. We had drudged for two solid hours so conscientiously that our arms swung in a natural sweeping action even without the brushes. Just then, the inspector, who had no evidence to confirm this, drove up the hill and halted by us.

'Now, lads! Don't let the force down. If you're going to sit idle in public, at least hide the barrow and look as though you belong to the waterworks.'

'We're only 'avin a breather.'

'Well, when you can spare five minutes, can you clear up some of that shale in Pall Mall. I've just come through there and there's more of it there now than in the car park.'

Pall Mall lay at the bottom of the car-park at the back of the 'Co-op' — a piece of gawdy Victorian architecture with the ugliest chimney in South Yorkshire poking out of it like a dirty cup and saucer stuck on a pedestal. Mike was not exaggerating. The flood had brought down enormous quantities of red shale, spilling them over the road like a still sea. It seemed more of a job for Moses than for us, especially as there was now less than an hour in which to finish it. Nevertheless we waded in, sweeping like madmen, and soon the air was filled with dust, to the sound of grunts and groans and the whispering rhythm of the brushes and the jarring crunch of the shovels. The bizarre music became faster and faster as our time grew short and volleys of stone shot hurtled into the bins with ever increasing hostility. There seemed to be no end to it, no bottom to the hollows the chippings had filled. But eventually it was done, the last scrapings slithered over the smouldering heap, and conveniently so, for the bins were so full that the lids only just fitted over them. It had been a mammoth task. Even Tug felt the strain.

'If Ah ever wake up an' find it rainin' like that again, Ah'll send our lass straight down wi' mi resignation.'

By now, we were late in setting back for the yard. Tug started off urgently along the causeway. As I had gained more practice that

day, I was left holding the reins. In equal haste, I pushed off to
catch up with him. But nothing moved. Again and again I tried but
without budging an inch — and no wonder, for there must have
been nearly eight cubic feet of solid rock pushing the other way.
Hasten slowly! I reasoned, coaxed, pleaded and finally promised
unspeakable reprisals, but the barrow was stone-deaf to it all.
Gallantly, Tug returned to assist and it was only then, by a
tremendous joint effort, that the two wheels roused themselves into
what at a close glance could be described as motion. Like Trojans
we sweated, groaned and fought our way up the hill. Grudgingly,
the barrow gave way, though it wrestled defiantly for every inch we
took.

As we turned down into New Street, the barrow sensibly ceased
to resist. That was the end of the struggle. That was the signal that
the rest of the journey was plain-sailing. That was why Tug released
his grip of the handle. That was why I began to run down the hill
attached to a hand-cart charging after a bread van and intent on
killing us both. Through fast-moving traffic we weaved — with the
barrow in full control of the steering — traffic that appeared to
assume, if the hooting was anything to go by that it was just an
irresponsible prank. Shoppers stopped, stared and shouted (much
more politely than the drivers). Soon I was running as fast as I have
ever done. Done in the proper place it would have been excellent
training for an Olympic sprinter wanting to cut down those vital
split-seconds.

'Stop it!' advised Tug helpfully, several yards in the rear.

In fact the thought had already occurred to me. Earlier in the day
I had noticed that the barrow rested on a limb suspended beneath
the front container. With our joint careers depending on it slowing
us down, I tilted the carriage forward to bring the front in contact
with the road. The sturdy prop proved, when an inspection was
more convenient, to be a small wheel, which explained why the
braking power seemed at the time to be extraordinarily inefficient.
Just then, however, as we streaked towards the busy junction with
Sheffield Road, with the traffic lights against us, the reasons for its
failure seemed of rather minor importance. My heels were gouging
inches out of the tarmac — and vice versa — and yet I might as well
have pushed for the difference I made. Then, to my intense relief,
Tug's broad hands appeared round the handle-bar. Had it not been

for his intervention, the barrow and I should have wasted little time in welding ourselves to the side of a bus. As it was, we came to a halt with the wheels resting on the white stop line and both of us feeling like men brought down from the rack for a tea-break.

This was all very well, but unfortunately, it was happening on the crown of the road, which is a somewhat unconventional position to take up when you want to turn left, and downright silly if a packed column of cars builds up on the inside indicating a right turn. Tug hopefully put out his left hand, but it was quite plain from the driver's expressions that they had no intention of giving way to a dustman's barrow which had recently tried to wrap itself round their rear bumpers. Our only chance lay in making for Primrose Hill, a gennel* immediately opposite which ran into Pontefract Road — and reaching it before someone attempted to clip our wings. The engines roared angrily and we crouched, heels raised, every nerve tensed. Red; red and amber! Not even Silverstone had witnessed such acceleration. Two corporation sweepers and one yellow hand-cart all but literally flew over the road before their nearest rival had even released the handbrake. Faster than hawks we sped, if not quite so gracefully. We pounded for the safety of the far kerb and thankfully felt the arm-shattering jolt as the barrow rose out of the gutter and leapt on to the pavement, while the high-pitched screams of fury and frustration swept behind us and passed away up the hill.

Troubles, they say, come in threes. The impact of hitting the kerb had done little to slow us down but had sent the barrow bouncing over the cobbles completely out of control. The narrow passageway now confined us and to our utter dismay had blocked our exit with an old man swaying on a knobbly, crooked walking-stick. The barrow, sensing blood, bolted for him, straining at the leash. We bore down on him with terrifying speed. Manoeuvring was impossible. Even the figure before us did nothing to help himself, but stood and gaped wide-eyed at his impending doom, regretting that he had troubled himself with the Beecham's Powder the night before. We skidded to a halt inches away from the shining toecaps of his boots. The two brushes that were laid on the flanks of the barrow slid out on either side of him and deftly

*Passage.

removed his stick. The shovels narrowly avoided slicing off his feet.

He did not offer his thanks for saving his life. He did not compliment our precision and timing. Instead, he was moved to a passionate speculation regarding both our histories from the circumstances of conception to the time when our secret inclinations could contain themselves no longer. Young hooligans! We had less sense than his dog, and he was dead. Playing games like that at our age; trying to frighten decent, bloody folk. In his day we would have been horsewhipped and sent to the trenches. It was his firm belief that another instalment of the Great War might teach some people to grow up.

By the time our barrow trundled laboriously into the yard the others were already queueing up in front of the inspector's office and the bell in the wooden porch was going beserk.

'Where shall we tip this stuff?' shouted Tug.

Stan emerged from the office. His was the mournfully sober sort of face that made him automatic choice for milk-monitor at school. It was a natural progression to inspector's right-hand man.

'What is it tha's got?'

'Crown Jewels!' replied Tug, sharply. 'A chap i' ' market sold 'em us cheap.'

Stan, not a gullible person, made a careful inspection and then directed us to a small pile of rubbish on the far side of the yard, and two men were persuaded to assist us. It took every ounce of strength of the four of us to unload the bins.

'What possessed thee to fill 'em this full?' said Charlie, gasping and snorting as we upended the second one. 'Tha gets no prizes for effort 'ere.'

'' i'spector told us to clear ' grit up be'ind "Co-op".'

'Tha should 'ave gied 'im a shovel then, shouldn't they, Fred? 'E wouldn't 'ave got me doin' it, Ah can tell thee.'

'He seemed such a nice man.'

'Tha might 'ave broke ' axle wi' that load on. Tha should nivver 'ave ' bins more na a third full, i'nt that reight, Fred?'

'Perhaps we should take two-thirds back.'

'Tha could 'ave damaged us backs just now. If tha does it again Ah'm not 'elpin' thee. What's tha say, Fred?'

Fred lazily surveyed the distant skies, carefully assessing our performance.

'Damn silly buggers, Ah say.'

3 The Cardboard Lorry

We stood under the barrow shed, Tug and I, watching the steady trickle of duffle jackets and blue overalls shuffling into the depot like drooping zombies, directed by unseen forces to the little porch to pay homage to that impassive-faced clock which was master of us all. To them all its penetrating voice made a curt acknowledgement. Ping! Ping! Somehow the bell seemed deliberately to ring louder and shriller in the morning, when nerves are tender and the slightest sound is torture to the ear. How it enjoyed its brief importance; with sneering insolence it taunted our sore, enfeebled minds. No doubt if it had been capable of feeling pain to the slightest degree, many of its victims would then and there have derived untold pleasure from slowly dismembering it.

This was as it always was. Every day, before the small red van rumbled across the yard to herald the start of a bright new working day, we sheltered under the eaves, perhaps hoping that if we did not consider the event it would never happen. In this fashion we spoke on all manner of subjects from Tug's verruca to a dustman's standing in society, from the chances of putting a man on the moon to the more remote chances of Barnsley winning the FA Cup, punctuating our discussions with wide yawns of ignorance, lack of interest and exhaustion. Even yawning before seven o'clock of a morning seemed to consume a wholly unnecessary amount of precious energy. Tug would lean against a steel upright, his packed lunch protruding from the front pocket of his overalls, like a kangaroo that had surprised itself. I argued more comfortably if supported by a dust-cart. Together we hammered out enormous problems in these sessions — Tug's feet cleared up before the end of August, although there seemed little change in the dustmen's condition. That was as it always was.

Here we met Laughing Gus. You had only to look at him to be

amused. His gaunt figure bowed low beneath the weight of his clothing. A pair of enormous boots, in which his feet must have wandered like lost souls, anchored him to Mother Earth in a high wind. After years of successful cultivation his shoulders had almost joined together in front of him. Above all, he wore a smile like other people wear suits: perhaps he even kept it on in bed.

'Ah went to Blackpool for mi 'olidays. Lovely room they gave mi. Fit for gentlemen. It said so on ' door.'

He paused to laugh.

'Ah 'ad to go to ' doctor's while Ah were there. Ah says, "Ah'm 'avin' trouble wi' mi breathin', Doc." 'E says, "Reight, old love. Ah'll gie thee summat to stop it."'

His frail body succumbed to fits of mirth. Tears ran down his cheeks. Gus enjoyed a joke more than any other person I have ever known, and was not in the least inhibited by the fact that they were all his own. His hoarse cackle echoed around the yard and the walls trembled like the walls of Jericho.

It was Tug who first suggested that, really, Gus was lonely, who observed that he must browse through every magazine, sit through every comedy programme, and absorb every quip so that his timid, lonely being could crawl from its dark, cold world with access to the comfort of friendly ears. Until then I had never realized that laughter and crying are often just two faces of the same coin. But afterwards I saw that, no matter how heartily he was laughing, his eye never ceased to watch the reaction of his audience. And the lines on his face revealed more than middle-age.

'So Ah says to mi Mam, Ah says, "Ah feel we're in for some brass this week. Ah've started doin' ' pools." She says, "That's no sign o' money. It just means tha're drinkin' too much".'

Joss had not turned up for work that morning. He was driver's mate in one of the cardboard lorries. According to a binner who lived in the same street, the man was in bed with his back again. Due sympathy for this distressing condition circulated around those now pressing to take his place. For many years he had served in the Royal Navy until one night when he returned to his ship very drunk, jumped into his hammock which some unkind friends had removed, and broke his back. Now he wore a brace to support the entire length of his spine, although he insisted that the frigate had had the worst of it.

Somehow I was selected as his replacement, and shortly afterwards I was sitting beside Harry Jagger, the driver, as we rode out of the yard to our first port of call. There were two cardboard lorries; one a medium-sized covered van, ours a small tipping lorry, low-sided but fenced in at the front and sides by a seven-foot-high wire cage to increase its loading capacity. Our crew of two was supplemented by Bessie, a buxom, hardboard wench who sat on top of the cabin clutching a tumbling horde of butter, cheese, yoghurt and other dairy produce in her fat arms. Joss and Harry had a deep affection for this lovely creature and even provided her with a plastic mackintosh for rainy days.

The function of these particular vehicles was to collect the empty cardboard boxes, containers, paper rolls and packing from the shops, and deliver them to the Corporation depot at Pogmoor where it would be sold as salvage to be reprocessed. Collection was normally made on a weekly basis, save for the larger stores — especially the supermarkets — whose larger turnovers and lack of accommodation demanded daily removals. It was to Lipton's supermarket that we drove first. There was no-one about in the enclosure when we arrived, but what it lacked in people it more than made up for in the vast quantities of cardboard boxes that soared above us in precarious mountains. My heart wept at the affluence of modern society, only to be consoled when Harry got out of the cab to help me. The drivers were under no obligation to lend a hand, but nearly all of them did, because, as Harry said, it was less tiring than watching a work-mate struggling on his own. In this way, instead of the task taking two hours, we bundled them all into the back of the lorry within twenty minutes. And by then, it was half-past eight and 'snap-time'.

Even as we screeched to a halt outside the canteen, we could see that the place was not lacking in workers to occupy it. 'Snap-time' was officially twenty minutes, but in order to promote safe and comfortable digestion, it had been unofficially extended to a more realistic forty minutes, and if those in authority in the Town Hall did not object they had only their own ignorance to blame. We sat in the corner by the window. The room reeked of disinfectant.

"As Nasty Nigel done it again?'

Norman, mop in hand, appeared from the lavatories.

'Not 'afe! Don't worry though. 'E got to ' bog this time. 'E just couldn't get 'is breeches down fast enough.'

'Is 'e still there?'

'No! They've sent 'im ome.'

'Not on ' bus, I 'ope!'

''E's walkin' it. An' 'e's left a trail o' shit from 'ere to 'is 'ouse.'

Harry unwrapped his food-pack, but not with peckish enthusiasm.

'If 'e ever does it while Ah'm 'ere, Ah'll sew 'is arse up. 'E ruins
mi snap every time. It took mi ten year to learn our lass that there's
other things 'sides cheese to put in mi sandwiches an' Ah can't
remember now when they didn't taste as though she'd sprinkled
Dettol on 'em.'

Savagely, he tore into his bread and cheese.

'Where's thi snap, kid?' he asked.

'I didn't bring any.'

'That's no way to put weight on.'

'I had an egg before I came out.'

'Tha can cook, then?'

'No. I ate it raw.'

'Tha're kiddin' mi.'

'No. I always eat them raw in a morning.'

'Well, tha're damned 'eathen, then! Oi! Fred! Basil! Mi mate
'ere eats raw eggs.'

''E's 'avin' thee on.'

'That's what Ah told 'im, but 'e won't 'ave it.'

Meanwhile, a van had drawn up outside the canteen. It was like
the inspector's except that it was fitted with a ventilator on the
roof. The driver came in with a small brown paper parcel tucked
under his arm, and his work-mates parted respectfully to give him
free passage down the aisle. He took his seat alone in the corner
opposite our own.

'Who's he?'

'' bug man.'

'What's his line?'

'Well, tha sees: 'e cleans aht dirty 'ouses. Say tha's got a 'ouse
that's full o' lice or cockroaches or vermin; its 'im as comes an'
fumigates ' place aht for thee. That van's loaded wi' poison. That's
why 'e 'as that ventilator; otherwise 'e'd choke 'issen.'

'Isn't he very popular then?'

''Ow does tha mean? 'Course 'e is: one o' ' best.'

'Why does he sit on his own then?'

'Ah've told thee — 'e's ' bug man.'

'You mean, because he comes in contact with lice, no-one will come in contact with him?'

'That's it ... Tha can sit wi' 'im if tha wants — Ah'm not stoppin' thee. But tha're not gettin' back i' ' cab till Norman's disinfected thee.'

We left the bug man in his lonely cocoon. Our duties called us back to the supermarkets, that land of bargain prices, Green Shield stamps and cold impersonality. Altogether we must have visited half a dozen of them in the day, yet with the regular, grill pattern of the gangways, nicely positioned displays, packed shelves, the clockwork cashiers whose fingers ran so efficiently over the keys, it was possible to imagine that we wandered through the same doors six times. Harry knew all the assistants, and they greeted him with cheery friendliness. Even more usefully, they took a full share in loading the lorry.

'Where's Joss?' asked Sally, a tall, willowy blonde.

'Laikin'. Bad back again. Nowt that a day in bed won't cure.'

'All depends 'ow 'e spends it, don't it? Who's yer friend?'

'College boy. Workin' in 'is 'olidays, like.'

'Doesn't say much, does 'e? Don't they talk at college?'

''E's all reight.'

'Ah think 'e's shy.'

'Per'aps yer can cure 'im.'

'Cheeky sod!'

But Harry could not contain his concern as we drove across Barnsley in between calls.

'Tha's got to chat ' birds up, kid or tha'll get nowhere. That's ' way they're bred, tha sees. They might be as randy as 'ell, but they still like to be coaxed a bit; they want to feel tha's fancied 'em 'cos tha're talkin' to 'em: it fair brings colour to their tits. They're all t' same all ovver ' world, choose who they are. Once they get goin', there's no stoppin 'em, but it's up to thee to turn ' tap on first. Don't be put off by them 'oity-toity college lasses buggerin' thee abaht. They might treat thee like muck, but 'afe on it's all show 'cos they daren't own up. Tha sees, it don't matter 'ow 'igh an' mighty they try to be, or 'ow prim an' proper: they all want t' same thing i' ' end an' it's thee what's got it, not them. Tha wants to forget that lot an' get stuck in wi' these girls. Tha'll be all reight wi' some on 'em. There's nowt fancy abaht 'em, no pretendin'. But tha's got to talk to 'em though — don't matter what tha says — just make 'em feel sexy. Tell a lass she's beautiful an' she'll lap it up, even if she's got a face like monkey snot. It's like throwin' thi dog scraps; 'e follows thi round then i' case tha's summat else. Women are just t' same. Say owt nice to 'em; then they feel noticed an ' they'll do owt for more.'

'But you've been doing this all morning and got nowhere.'

'Ahh, well! Ah'm married now wi' kids as old as them. It's not as important when tha're gettin thi oats regular. Ah just do it for fun, keep in practice, like. But Ah'm not sayin' Ah wouldn't 'ave taken it serious at thy age 'ad things been different. Pluck apples while they're ripe, Ah say ... Now there's a girl in this shop we're bahn to that's dyin' to 'ave a go at Joss, but Ah can't leave 'im alone 'cos of 'is bad back. Tell thi what; Ah'll gie thee five minutes alone wi' 'er afore Ah come in.'

A little later on, we headed for a fashion shop in the town centre.

'Tha sees ' manageress — that woman who's just come aht o' t' shop. Tha'd be all reight there. She'll take 'em down for anyone.'

'She must be at least forty.'

'That's what a young lad like you wants — a bit o' experience. An' 'er assistant — that blonde girl wi' t' red mini skirt — she's a reight raver. Tha can guarantee whenever tha're comin' up ' stairs, she'll be at ' top of 'em bendin' o'er. Ee, we've made some trips down t' cellar, me an' Joss. Thee watch.'

As the morning progressed and we travelled here and there around the borough, I acquired a working knowledge of the moral inclinations of almost all the girls who served behind a counter. This one was 'stuck-up': that one was 'anybody's for a rum-and-black'. Neither the manageress nor her blonde helper came up to form, nor were the many others whose virtue was reputed to be the cheapest item in the shop bent on their particular pleasures as we entered their lairs, but Harry was in no way put out by the general apathy. His authority remained unimpaired. We knew the sordid history of the girl in the shoe shop, and all her affected innocence, so faultlessly displayed, could not obliterate the stark truths of her riotous youth. The secret passion of the plump cashier for half the manual force in Barnsley was common knowledge within the Cleansing Department. Well might she prattle on about her husband's sinus trouble: she had six children, each with differently coloured hair. No doubt, they, like others who found two lives more exciting than one, assured themselves that they deceived society as easily as they did those most close to them, but little misleads an observant neighbour and even less excites his shrewd perception.

For similar reasons, the women in a large number of local works and factories were always a popular topic of conversation in the depot canteen. Apparently, the type of industry and the place in which a woman worked provided a nearly perfect test of her virtue, and measured her sexual appetite on a chart that was orally passed round to every male interested in research. Presumably, if she changed her job her principles adjusted themselves to the new situation. To be accepted by certain firms she had to be as susceptible to manly charms as a block of reinforced concrete. By contrast, the most notorious business in the district employed 300 women in 200 jobs by a system closely resembling feudal crop-rotation: at any one time a third were pregnant but working, a third were rearing their latest offspring at home and the rest, now back to work, lay fallow. These were certainties: the rest were calculated gambles, normally with the odds heavily in the punter's favour.

Half-a-dozen times or more we travelled up to Pogmoor with cardboard brimming over the tall, wire cage. Not that it was difficult work; throwing empty, cardboard boxes on to a lorry is not an exercise likely substantially to develop one's physique. Indeed, at Tesco's, there were so many staff to assist us that it was almost necessary to apologize for doing it at all. What were not so agreeable, however, were the sorry deposits behind the little, street shops. Sodden, heavy, tearing under the slightest pressure and sometimes heavily laced with broken glass, they produced oaths of such intense strength as is not likely to be forgotten on Judgement Day.

The last load of the morning came from two chemist's shops in the shopping centre. Most of it was unopened stock from the cellars that had been damaged by the flood. We rushed back to the depot with a bonaza worth hundreds of pounds and distributed the spoils to the others in the canteen during lunch hour. Men streamed on and off the lorry to salvage for their wives or girl friends several years' supply of lipstick, rouge, hand cream, corn pads, shampoo, perfume, powder, linament and sticking plaster, regardless of how they were to get love-tokens in such bulk home. They searched pockets of mud for tissues and jars of baby food, and greedily hunted down every single, soggy toilet roll, thinking to dry them out in the gas oven or around the dining-room fire. If water had seeped into the nail varnish, no matter: there was so much more. Norman claimed a whole carton of toothpaste, in spite of only having his back molars left, simply because he enjoyed eating it. By the end of half an hour, the lorry had been cleared of everything except cartons, broken bottles, paper which had turned into mush and tubes and containers spilling out hair vitaliser, shaving cream and dried milk.

This sorry residue was fit only for the refuse tip. We set off in that direction immediately after lunch. On the way, Harry took us on a short detour and brought the lorry to a halt at his front gate. Tuesday, it seemed, was a day on which he made his egg deliveries. He had hit upon the enterprise after his vegetable crops had failed for three successive years and when even the weeds were refusing to grow. At the far end of his garden he had erected a moderately-sized hen-run and stocked it with thirty or forty Rhode Island Reds. Not surprisingly, he found customers all over Barnsley for his cheap, free-range eggs, and in order to keep low the costs of carriage he delivered his orders by the cardboard lorry. We stacked five dozen or more on the engine bonnet inside the cab. On his final trip, however, Harry returned with just a single egg and a large, blue mug. He thrust them both into my hands.

'Sithee! Ah want to see thee eat it.'

'Which?'

'Ah want to see thee eat a raw egg.'

'But I'm not hungry. We've only just eaten fish and chips.'

'Tha can manage this. Go on!'

He spoke as if he intended to thrust it down my throat, shell and all, if I refused, so it seemed best to oblige him while his hospitality lasted. Harry looked on with a mixture of awe and disgust until I had finished.

'An' don't tha feel sick after that?' he asked, sternly.

I shook my head.

'Well, Ah bloody do, now!' he yelled. 'Just don't let me catch thee doin' that again ... Tha're not reight in thi 'ead, does tha know? God! If tha worked wi' me every day Ah'd go balmy.'

All the way down Littleworth Lane Harry fought against the lorry's attempts to set a new land-speed record. Its engine whined and choked alternately with frustration. Below us and to our left lay the tip. It was an ugly sight and any apology that refuse heaps are not intended, primarily, to be beautiful would have provided little consolation to the people on whose back gardens it threatened to encroach. The houses in Lundwood Estate clung together in a rough, close-knit, oval shape, depressing and dingy with the filth that the winds blew over them, and brooded resentfully over the uncomfortable fate of being the dustbin for every other community in the borough. On the hill above them, Monk Bretton Colliery spewed out mountains of mud and slack from the bowels of the earth, creating an equally vile eyesore. While others beyond these mutilated hills basked in the still warmth of that glorious July, Lundwood sulked between two foul wastes, one being buried, the other exhumed. Tall chimneys on the hillside belched poisonous smoke clouds into stagnant air until, like grotesque mushrooms spreading their festering caps, they shrouded the ailing valley, starving it of sunlight and the beauty of the deep-blue skies, and all the while their sooty spores rained down contemptuously on the homes of those who served them. It seemed a heavy price to pay, but dirt and despoliation are the necessary evils of a mining community. What was so unfortunate for Lundwood was that it suffered the unsightly slack-heap of its own wastes on one side and the tip of everybody else's on the other.

The older part of the tip down by Pontefract Road had been covered with topsoil and turned into a playing area. Close by the estate were swings, the roundabout and the slide on which little children indulged themselves in the pleasures of motion until the local gang of adolescents chased them away and demolished whatever they could. A cricket pitch, marked out with bricks stacked up as a wicket and an untidy pile of coats at the bowler's end, occupied the centre of the intervening green. We turned in at the gate opposite the school and followed the black river that flowed across the upper part of the tip towards its wide and turbulent estuary. Waves of mud cascaded over deep troughs scarred by the bites of lorry tyres, and our vessel pitched and rolled aross the tortured wastes threatening every minute to capsize. Here and there tins, bottles, pieces of plastic tossed overboard during previous voyages, lay smeared and half-pressed beneath the surface. Shreds of paper whirled about in our wake like seagulls circling round the trawler sailing into home port.

There were several vehicles already there on the far side, some riding idly at anchor, others in the motions of discharging their stinking cargoes. One of the dustbin lorries was there, its great, silver body pivoted on the chassis and pointing to the sky in an awesome, magnificent salute. As we tacked our way towards this flotilla dozen or so boys miraculously acquired form from a few heaps of rubbish and raced as if for their lives in our direction. They were dirty, scruffy boys, in dirty, well-worn clothes, with matted hair and grimy hands and knees, boys of all ages, boys who at that moment were supposed to be enjoying the benefits of free, state education. Apparently, this type of free education proved more profitable. As they reached the back of the wagon, they swung themselves over the tailboard with expert ease, careless of the intrinsic difficulties most people would encounter in an instantaneous change of velocity from ten miles an hour in one direction to twenty miles an hour in the other. And once mounted, all the violent bucking and bouncing of the lorry could not dislodge them. With feverish swiftness they sifted through the debris regardless of the shattered glass and the loose razor blades, intent only on the discovery of a fortune thrown away while keeping a wary eye on the good luck of their companions. Occasionally, one of them would catch hold of something with a cry of 'Brass' or 'Got some lead!' and stuff it into his pockets. It was not a good load this time, but they managed to retrieve several shillings'-worth of scrap metal. Not yet in their teens, they could already identify every common metal and alloy at a glance: they even distinguished metal coated with paint, apparently by its weight. Doubtless too they could quote current prices and haggle on an equal basis with the shrewdest of metal brokers.

About a score of men were standing on the fringes of the tip. Some of them I recognized — a few drivers, the tip foreman and his son. But the rest were strangers, shuffling about in the refuse, heads down, shoulders bent, now and then glancing suspiciously around them and seeming more often than not angered by what they saw.

One by one the rubbish-heaps were being swept over the edge by a large, yellow bulldozer. It was something of a surprise to see a woman at the wheel of this unwieldly machine, but no man could have driven it with greater skill. She was a beautiful woman, Jenny, with long, red hair draped over her shoulders and large, dark eyes. Strange it was, in a world where wealth or beauty could travel as sure an upward path as did talent, that such a face should be abandoned to such desolation. And stranger still, she appeared to be content.

The smell was nauseating. Mouldy paper, rotting vegetation and thousands of similarly unsavoury spoils gave off a combined odour of peculiar foulness that would have all but paralysed a normal breathing apparatus. It was the only time I ever went as far as the dumping area, save for the days when it rained too hard for me sensibly to wait at the exit into Littleworth Lane. The place must have been literally crawling with disease and yet here were people, at whose age I had gone down with mumps, chicken pox and measles merely through knowing the cousin of someone who was infected, wandering around completely unscathed. Much later, someone told me that though they might be hardy in their youth their natural resistance to infections would be exhausted before they reached middle-age. Then, however, it seemed incredible.

Loaded with spoils from the wagons, the boys would scamper back to their fathers to hand it over with a curious mixture of meekness and pride. If there was any parental joy derived from seeing the fruits of their offspring's efforts, none was displayed. Like diamond merchants they scrutinized the junk with a critical eye, and almost with indifference dropped those pieces that were of value into a grubby sack or a shabby bag. Praise would not increase their worth.

A small, curly-headed boy of about six stumbled up to the totter* nearest us, his little fists clutching a prize of seemingly enormous costliness.

'What's tha got?' asked his father, gruffly, and snatched it from

*Scavenger.

him before he could form an answer.

'Lead!' replied the boy, dutifully. 'An' bloody 'eavy. Ah put it i' mi pocket an' it tore a 'ole through an' landed on mi foot.'

Instantly his father smacked him hard across the face. There was not a whimper from the lad, not a movement — except for the initial recoil — not even to bow his head.

'Careless pig! Tha's not fit to 'ave clothes. Well tha're not gettin' any more till tha's worn 'em aht, Ah'm tellin' thee now. An' if tha does it again Ah'll 'ave ' belt to thee.'

The boy tossed back his curls.

'Is this all tha's brought?'

'Ah couldn't 'old any more.'

An even heavier blow sent him down on his knees.

'What's tha laikin' at, stupid bugger? There's all them buggers yon sortin' aht, an' tha's left 'em to it just to bring mi a lump o' bloody lead. Tha's 'ad it now, kid. It's ' belt for thee toneet. Get back there, an' don't come back baht bloody jewels.'

His erring child limped across the furrowed earth towards the group of boys busily looting a jumbled mass of garbage. The marks of his beating hardly coloured his dirty, pale face, as though he had become immune to punishment through its frequent application. He seemed at peace with his world.

''Avin' trouble, Sid?' Harry asked the totter.

'Arr! Actin' fool all day. Ah'll lace 'im though when Ah get 'im 'ome, little arse.'

'Tha didn't take that job they sent thee, then?'

'Nivver went. Ah sent our lass to tell 'em Ah were badly.'

'Tha'll get fun aht, tha knows. One o' these days, ' Government'll say, "Old Sid's not workin'," an' send someone down to thee.'

'Sod ' Government! Any'ow, they'll 'ave to catch mi in first.'

Sid spat on the side of the lorry and moved away. Harry looked at me and shook his head, but his expression was beyond understanding. The totters were moving across the path of another vehicle being tossed and shaken by the black storm at the mouth of the tip. They seemed to belong to the tip, these grim, silent men, as much as the plagues of flies that swarmed over the filth and the rotting waste. We saw them there, day after day, fair weather or foul, scratching around the piles of refuse like human carrion.

Occasionally, when a police patrol car appeared on Littleworth Lane, they would vanish into the earth, but as soon as it climbed away towards Monk Bretton, they were there again in force, hurling abuse and dark, savage threats. No-one was ever caught, and perhaps it was all a game whose rules did not allow it to happen, for otherwise their presence was tolerated, and the few shillings'-worth that they eked from the garbage went with them unchallenged.

How sad it seemed, and yet they did not look sorry for themselves. Perhaps that is what Harry meant; that, if it was a poor life, it was their choice. You think of the comparative comforts of modern living; you think of all the forces at work in the community running on a social conscience and of the rewards that come from steady employment: yet as night follows day, while they dump rubbish at Lundwood, the totters will come to Littleworth Lane tip. Perhaps that is what he meant.

4 Pogmoor

'It's Poggy for thee.'

Only the third day and Stan threw these words casually at me like tasty titbits to a hungry bird. How often they would be repeated in the following weeks. How often of a morning I would lean against the inspector's office, trying to push it over on top of Stan who was inside, waiting with the dull patience of a convict with his head on the block listening for the swish of the axe, until Stan had enjoyed my discomfort to the full and came out to deliver the final blow. And then I would envy the man beheaded: at least he had the satisfaction of knowing he was dead. But I was bound for Pogmoor, and one day there passed like an age in Hell. They were terrible words, and even now their echo reeks of burning sorrow, sickliness and everything unholy. All that summer I held them in cold fear, and though as many days as not they came to lash my ears unmercifully, their sting never lost its fierceness and I heard them only with growing bewilderment. I should have run many miles to escape Stan's mocking overtones and their awful consequences had not reason, tottering on the brink of frenzy, rocked back on to its foundations. But on that first occasion I was not to know.

By now the mysterious ceremonies that were regularly performed every morning in the yard had paled into drab, predictable routine. The clocking-on, the waiting, the inspector's van, the procession of lorries that encircled the office like a pioneers' wagon train preparing to receive an Apache attack from Pontefract Road; it was the same, day in and day out, never changing, never ceasing.

But familiarity brings, by paradox, its own surprises. Slowly I was learning that there was a strict social order, even amongst dustmen and road-sweepers. Outsiders, through shining naivity, tend to group them all together on a particular rung on the social ladder — frequently the bottom one — and ignore the subtle distinctions conspicuous to anyone admitted to their order. But differences there are, and they very quickly become apparent.

The elite were the dustmen, 'the binners' as they were called. Everyone who felt the slightest flicker of ambition in his bones longed for the glorious day when he was elevated to their ranks to be borne past his lesser kin in his silver carriage. In accordance with their grand status they were paid the most princely wages at the rate of seven shillings and sixpence per hour, which explained why, whenever one of their number was absent, people were at each other's throats to replace him. But this was not their only, or even major, advantage. They were the only Council workers fortunate enough to work on a 'task' system; that is to say, they were given a fixed amount of work to do in a day, and when they had completed it, they went home while their wages were calculated on the basis of a forty-hour week. When the scheme was originally introduced the effect was staggering. Instead of men loitering around the streets all day with bins on their shoulders they were finishing, so the Town Hall was astonished to learn, at half-past eleven every day. Furthermore the majority of them were now working part-time in the afternoons in garages and workshops all over Barnsley, which provided a welcome boost to local industry without placing a corresponding burden on the Inland Revenue. When the unions agreed to adopt that system, they must have been laughing their heads off.

Foremost amongst the dustmen themselves was the Kendray team. Leaving the depot at half-past seven, the four of them would empty their quota of four hundred and thirty-two dustbins before ten o'clock every day — although on Fridays, when they looked forward to a long weekend, they finished a little earlier at half-past-eight. They ran from first to last with bins brimming full on their shoulders. To the regular crew, of course, it was no hardship, but some of those drafted in as temporary replacements swore that they would cut off their right arms before emptying dustbins in Kendray again. There was no place there for persons with weak hearts or short legs. Just to keep fit, the ganger* ran from his house to the depot a mile away, fully clothed and shod in

*Crew leader.

boots, in six minutes, and we would see him jog across the yard to the porch every morning at a minute to seven as though he lived just round the corner. But their speed sucked trouble into its slipstream. On that very day they were ordered to report to the Superintendent to answer yet another complaint. Apparently, one of them, sprinting round from the back of a bungalow with a bin on his back, had tripped over a spur in the crazy paving and flown, bin and all, through forty pounds'-worth of picture-window and returned the week's waste by distributing it all over the sitting room. The Borough Engineer, hearing the story on an extremely efficient grapevine, had been highly amused until he arrived home to find his wife still clearing up the mess. So, now, there was trouble indeed.

Everyone else who worked on the rest of the lorry fleet received the same wage as the binners, but unfortunately had to suffer the full forty-hour week before earning it. It was an odd collection of vehicles that came down to the depot every day: there were the cardboard lorries, a dustbin lorry with the old semi-cylindrical back now adapted as a weed sprayer; there was the spare wagon — an intriguing term that puzzled me for some time to come — and the gulley cleanser with the long suction pipe flapping against its side like a bloated elephant's trunk. During term time, there was also a van from the depot delivering school meals. It always seemed to me a rather perverse arrangement, leaving the supply of children's dinners to the refuse collectors, but as the appetising qualities of school meals had resulted in the lunch hour becoming widely known as 'troughtime', I took it to be a curious example of Town Hall humour.

Those who, because of disabilities, misconduct, laziness or hard luck, failed to find a place on the lorries fell into the pool of road-sweepers, who were paid just six shilings and ninepence an hour. Most of them struggled along pushing hand-carts with brushes and spades sticking out in all directions and falling off every fifteen paces, but as a mark of progress there were half-a-dozen or more electric carts in use, which made a sweeper's life much easier even if it failed to make it more industrious. One of them even had a cabin for the crew to sit in with an optimistic warning, printed on the dashboard, not to load the truck with more than a ton. It was a very popular choice on a rainy day.

For the residue, not even selected for so lowly a post, there were a number of jobs in the yard waiting or invented to soothe the conscience that could not accept wages for a day spent in idleness. You might find yourself spring-cleaning the canteen or bailing cloth in the shed or painting woodwork that had been painted so often it was not just weather-proof, but bullet-proof.

'It's Poggy for thee.'

It was the way Stan broke this news to Tug and me that made us feel that we were in some way privileged. A strange power in his voice made his words ring with applause and envy as though what he said could be linked with phrases like 'Bully for you!', or 'Lucky for some!'. His smile was as warm as tepid milk, but we had no reason then to doubt its sincerity. Probably, we even returned the smile.

'It's Poggy for thee.'

He opened the back doors of the inspector's van. By this time, Mike O'Grady, the inspector was always immersed in paper work so this particular drive had become Stan's daily duty — and, I suspect, pleasure. Like lambs to the slaughter Tug and I meekly entered and crouched down as comfortably as was possible under the low roof, with each other's knees sticking into our ears and seated on razor-keen shovel blades. We were glad of the ride, glad to be going Somewhere, and feeling so very superior to the plodding groups of road-sweepers that we saw through the little rear windows as we sped by. At Town End we turned up the hill and then along Pogmoor Road. Row after row of dull, red-bricked, terraced houses looked on sullenly as we passed. Winter Road, Winter Terrace, Winter Avenue ...

'Ah can see us bein' sorry we didn't put thicker coats on,' Tug predicted.

The road down through the salvage depot was not designed for the comfort of persons being driven in the back of a van, and we cursed every stone and hole in it while the shovels worked hard at our thighs and calves. Stan pulled up beside a row of buildings that looked suspiciously like the remains of a POW camp, and unlocked the back of the van. In abject surrender we got out and followed Stan into the end section, still nursing our wounds as decently as possible.

The room we entered was the mess-room, and rarely has a name been so appropriate. What light there was filtered through a tiny lobby, while the window was thick with grime, almost as solid as the walls themselves. Cupboards, cardboard boxes, tins of paint and curtain rods sported themselves around the room in gay abandon, festooned with grimy pyjamas and plastic raincoats. The walls were black except where tears of rain, seeping from the roof, carved whitewashed, schizophrenic paths like snails on a church-yard path. A pretty, blonde girl, pressed against a cupboard, had charitably attempted to brighten the dingy surroundings by taking off her clothes, but an anonymous Philistine had abused her good nature by treating certain areas of her beauty as a God-given design for long-range darts practice. There was such squalor here as had never known the scourge of a woman's broom, where a man could sink instantly into a warm sea of blissful ease, free to trail in as much dirt as cared to accompany him and careless whether he creased that spotless headrest or dropped ash in the sugar basin.

'Oi! Two more for thee, Jeth,' said Stan.

Jeth looked over last January's copy of *The Beano* and through his feet, which were polishing the table, and scowled.

'Student! They've sent another student. Aren't we reight 'ere, now then?'

Various comics collapsed to reveal three anguished faces which shook themselves and spat appropriately.

'There aint no-one else bar these two,' Stan apologized.

'Well, don't blame me when ' machine seizes up again,' Jeth warned him.

He sighed and reached for the pencil and paper on the table.

'What's thi names, then?'

'Tug Spooner.'

The revelation seemed too mediocre to fire in Jeth the necessary inspiration. He sat, pen in hand, like a poet trying to improve his last line.

''Ow's tha spell it?'

'T ... U ... G ... ?'

But Jeth had still not moved.

''Ow does tha write "T"?'

'' same as everyone else. Can't tha write or summat?'

'Can 'e buggery,' said Stan. 'Tha should see ' fun an' games we 'ave wi' ' time sheets 'e sends down. There's folks on sometimes we've nivver 'eard on.'

The whole site had originally, so Jeth told me, been a gigantic stone quarry, gouged forty feet deep into the earth, and had given many a young child the irresistible opportunity to throw himself to his death. Even when the waters had all but risen to the brim, they came, stubbornly determined, to drown like lemmings. Hearkening to the complaints of an ageing population, the Corporation gave it several years' life as a rubbish dump and then built the salvage depot on it. The present generation on the neighbouring estate bore little gratitude for its salvation. Round the bottom side ran a railway shunting line where convoys of ancient wagons squealed to and fro at a snail's pace and scraped inches off one's nerves in a matter of days. And everywhere there was litter, on the grass, on the roads, on the railway line, tin cans, cardboard sheets and plastic bags, placid enough on a breathless, sultry day but viciously aggressive in a high wind.

We never began work until the first lorry arrived with its load of cardboard, and then we would emerge from the hut like men awakened from a long sleep (which was often the case), and stumble across to the depot works, a tragic monument of brick and sheets of corrugated iron. It was normally half-past-eight by this time and the early sun was pouring streams of pale, pure gold through the holes in the roof. Jeth would kneel down by the machine and turn levers, curse and sweat, stand up and kneel down again and pull pieces of cord, until the sleeping beast, choked by his cigarette smoke, stirred into life and we would watch them coughing and spluttering together in sheer exhaustion. I remember learning on a stack of cardboard on the first day, watching this going on, and out of the corner of my eye seeing a square yard of thick, steel plate rush out of the gaping mouth of the press and hurl itself at me. Rigid with shock, I felt it crush body and soul out of my armrest and start to pound away at it with relentless, maniacal fury. Then the air became thick with the feverish ramblings of the monster as it shook the grooves that shackled it and the gasps of the unfortunate cardboard as its breath was brutally squeezed from it. Clouds of dust heaved in torment to the skies; paper and celluloid gripped by teeth of iron and brick flapped feebly in their vain efforts to escape, and the dim-lit world descended into an inferno of chaos, storm and quaking.

The procedure was quite simple. The cardboard lorries left their cargoes at the top entrance (which, since the building was hard against the edge of the old quarry, was halfway up the inside wall). Ernie dragged it forward and pushed it down the chute. The Old Man stood at the bottom to prevent the chute from becoming clogged, and spat. The hammer drew back beneath the chute and rammed whatever fell into its path into the body of a cardboard bale. As this heaving larva gorged itself to a length of three feet, Jeth stood by to bind it with fascinating speed and skill and wheel it off to the store. It was a highly efficient system of work and marvellous to watch, which we did. In fact, it was transparently plain that the last thing it required was assistance from Tug and me.

'Oi! Tha two! Clear all that muck off o' ' motor.'

I was vaguely familiar with the employer's duty in law to fence the moving parts of a machine — a knowledge later reinforced when I was standing on a ladder replacing a board that patched up the upper wall and discovered on its reverse side a large notice explaining certain statutory regulations concerning safety at work — but evidently some manufacturers were less well acquainted. The most remarkable feature of this particular machine was that not a single action in it was guarded, even by another moving part. The motor, the transmission belt, the driving shaft and the piston were all frankly and defiantly exposed. Instead of slowly withdrawing behind a web of filth in a dark corner of Pogmoor it should have enjoyed pride of place as a model in a technical college laboratory. But there it was, and looking back, it did serve to teach us something that day. If ever there was a job to be done which, even there, was considered unpleasant; if ever anyone's fingers, eardrums or life had to be risked for the sake of the operation, Tug and I were left in no doubt as to whose would be considered the most expendable.

It took us nearly an hour to complete this first lesson, having been detained by the practical problems of unravelling polythene bags from a fan belt travelling at high speed. I had only just wheeled the barrow to the edge of the tip and thrown out its contents when Pat called us back again. He led us past the machine, through the store packed solid with cardboard bales, through a bay open to the winds after a fire the year before had removed the roof and now a treasure house of rubble, plastic bags, iron bars and mile upon mile of typing ribbon, and finally into the far room of the complex, a dark, dank, dingy cavern, from whose eerie recesses all light had fled. The floor was a sickly turmoil of reeking mulch that rose a good foot before the gloom devoured it. It was the sort of place you came across in a nightmare and woke up screaming, convinced of having just seen Hell.

'Clean this up afore tha goes today,' said Pat. 'Ah'm sick o' t' sight of it.'

'What is it?'

'Only cardboard what's fallen out o' ' bales. It'll not 'urt thee.'

'There's an awful lot of it!'

'Aye! Well! It's been 'ere ever sin' Ah come 'ere, an ' that's ovver five year ago.'

'Do you think the local archaeological society would be interested? It smells a lot older.'

'Nay, kid,' said Tug. 'That's ' bodies of them as suffocated tryin' to clean it last time.'

'Tha're both wrong. That's rat shit. Tha'd best make sure tha don't corner one when tha gets to ' end. Oi! come back in 'ere!'

In our speedy evacuation we had not troubled ourselves with the barrow, brushes or shovels. From the safety of the dusty tip we peeped back in through the great entrance to the open bay. Pat was not wearing his most winning expression.

'What kind of rats?' I asked, out of scientific interest.

'Big uns. Ah've seen some two foot long, includin' ' tail. They thrive on this 'ere cardboard; makes 'em breed like vermin.'

'Are there many of them?'

''Undreds. ' place's ovverrun wi' 'em. Jeth's dog, Mack, lives on 'em. Tha sees all that muck piled up in ' bay? — it's crawlin' wi' 'em. ' last time ' caterpillar came an' shifted that, it were pickin' thirty up i' ' bucket every time. They were fair pourin' aht.'

'Don't thee be afraid, nip,' said Tug when Pat had left us. 'If we see a rat tha can use mi shovel on it.'

'Why yours?'

''Cos Ah shall leave it 'ere wi' thee.'

The noise we made in that storehouse even drowned the machine at the other end of the building. We stamped our feet, shovels clattered about, we sang, whistled and shouted, not easy exercises when your chin rests on your chest to protect your throat. When sludge overflowed from the barrow, we were at pains to ensure that the other did not suffer under the burden of carrying it away alone. The smell grew progressively more rancid; mud oozed behind us over the newly-exposed stone floor; water dripped from the rafters with sinister sounds all about us; the cardboard whispered and hissed angrily as the steel blades severed it until sweat froze the clothes to our bodies; the darkness became darker as we ventured further in; but of the rats — or Mack — we saw never a sign.

The presence of Pat at the depot remained something of a mystery to me that summer. He was second in command to Jeth, although he never came down to work on the cardboard press. He operated a smaller press for bailing newspaper and magazines in a long building adjoining the mess hut, but because his output fell far below that of the combined efforts of the rest of us he was generally considered to be rather lazy. There was something strange about him, that crooked nose, those black eyes that glinted beneath the peak of his flat cap and shifted warily around him, missing nothing. When he spoke you were immediately on guard, slow to reply to prevent any possibility of misinterpretation, for it was said he told tales to the Superintendent. The others regarded him with a mixture of awe and fear, and he aggravated the situation when they dug out their favourite copies of *The Beezer* by exhibiting a preference for glossy, pornographic magazines. As rumour had it his wife was so ugly that during past power failures the abattoir had found her invaluable, and she had had to break Pat's nose before he submitted to propose to her. On Saturday evenings, they both made a tour of a few town stores and supermarkets, collected a week's supply of foods which had remained beyond the last selling date, and fed the whole family on a free diet of dainties considered unsafe for human consumption. He drove a three-wheeled motor-car built around a motor-bike engine he had found rotting on the tip: the entire body was composed of aluminium plates held together by glue and so many thousands of carpet tacks that at a distance it looked to have been sewn together. It was known that through these economic restrictions he had built up a large fortune, but he carried so little round with him that he was frequently compelled to borrow money for cigarettes.

Apart from a somewhat limited interest in photography, his only pleasure lay in tinkering with and talking about motor-cars, and in company with his fellow enthusiast, Jeth — and sometimes not — he spent many hours of a working day doing both. Jeth was the proud owner of a remarkable vehicle that began as a Hillman, went through several stages of Ford and rounded off as a Rover. Everyone in Pogmoor was well acquainted with its qualities, for Jeth had a voice that could knock a man unconscious at twenty paces. The only person for whom he would lower the volume was his wife; even then she was now partially deaf. Being the foreman he enjoyed the doubtful privilege of having living accommodation on site, next to the long building that housed the paper press. He had a simple, honest face that inspired trust in all who dealt with him coupled with a soul-searching frankness that constrained him persistently to describe his acquisition of almost everything he possessed — with the exception of his wife and children — as 'nicking from the tip'.

'Someone chucked a table on ' tip o' Saturday — good as new an' all,' he said.

We were sitting in the mess room patiently awaiting the end of the breakfast hour.

'Just what Ah wanted, so Ah nicked it. Tha'll nivver see a better one i' ' shops, now then.'

'Our George did mi car in good an' proper, tha knows,' Pat replied.

'Leg comes off our old un. Used to send us dinner flyin' all round ' room. It were dangerous.'

'Ah told 'im afore 'e got in to take them great boots 'e wears off, but 'e wouldn't 'ave it. So we're goin' up Race Common Road an' 'e puts 'is feet straight through ' floor.'

'It came off one day, an' ' table top landed reight on mi knees. Ah thowt it'd cut mi leg in 'afe. Ah couldn't walk reight for days.'

'Ah couldn't make out why ' car were suddenly goin' faster. Then Ah looks at 'im an' sees 'is feet peddlin' away like 'Ell.'

'Couldn't tha knock a nail in it?' asked Tug.

'' wood were split. An' glue wouldn't take, so Ah turned it round to ' wife's side.'

The rest of us listened in silence. The Old Man champed through the top half of his pile of strawberry jam sandwiches — his staple diet — his faded, watery eyes staring vacantly into the mists of time. Very occasionally he produced a few garbled oaths when someone or something displeased him, but generally the rest of creation seemed beyond his contemplation. I only once heard him utter a single word in an attempt to contribute to the conversation, but as someone slammed the door at that precise moment, this seasoned pearl of wisdom was shattered into dusty oblivion. According to Jeth he had never been outside the county borough in his entire life, considered tales of a large body of water called 'sea' to be absurd myths, and spent every holiday in bed. He never smoked, drank or married, the only thing from which he visibly derived any pleasure being a strawberry jam sandwich. He and Ernie resided at the same hotel, providing ample evidence that it was run on the lines of a silent order of monks. Few people were blessed with such an extensive sense of humour as Ernie was: he would break into muffled giggles merely telling someone the time. He was a keen reader of *The Dandy*, and had stacked in a corner of the mess room all his favourite copies dating back to 1952. His quiet reserve, however, did not obscure his friendly disposition, though he had an unnerving habit of carelessly throwing cigarette ends on to drifts of paper which collected across the exist, and you could not but notice the expression of vague innocence that flitted across his face whenever the fire that had recently gutted half the depot buildings was mentioned.

'Any'ow, when Ah fun this new un, Ah sold t'other to a mate.'

'What's thi mate want wi' a table wi' a gammy leg?'

'It's a good table, man — worth ten quid, easy, an' Ah only asked a fiver. Mind, Ah per'aps will mention about ' leg when Ah next see 'im, so as it's all above board, like.'

More often than not I was given the job of assisting Ernie to send salvage down the chute. It was very spasmodic work. For minutes on end we would stand in silence on the platform above the press, listening to its faultless, noisy rhythm and feeling the dust from the dry earth wafting across our faces. Then a lorry would arrive with up to half a ton of rubbish and deposit it in a great mound three or four feet high just outside the entrance. There was only one way of ensuring that we cleared it away before the next load came, and that was to wade into it, chest high, and with both feet and both hands or a long stick push forward large masses of it until they slipped down the slide. The effort almost drained you of the strength to stand. Just clearing a single load was as exhausting as a five-mile cross-country run — there cannot be many jobs where you go down with cramp after walking only twenty yards. At the same time we were supposed to see that only paper and cardboard passed down to the press, but it is hardly surprising that when we were both up to the neck in waste, our particular style of working did not lend itself to a scrupulous sifting process. We managed to throw out the odd bottle, and pull out long sheets of cellophane wrapping which promptly wrapped themselves around the machine under the platform, but often the first sign of foreign bodies was the ominous rattling of broken glass down the chute followed by a spate of furious cursing hurled in our direction by the Old Man, working at the bottom, as glass trickled up his sleeve. On the other hand, our superficial inspection frequently benefited those who were working below. Many a time Jeth would pick up something that had fallen out of the press, hold it triumphantly above his head, and in a voice effortlessly drowning the clamour of pistons and hammer shout, 'Ah've fun a tanner!' The frequency of these finds in no way diminished his excitement: every prize, be it only a penny, was worth a king's ransom. From the top of the chute Ernie would quietly disapprove of his unseemly exhibition. 'Only me an' mi pocket knows what Ah find,' he told me. Even the Old Man acquired a share of the loot, furtively extracting it from the passing river of seething chaos. Fortunes were lost and found in a jungle of cardboard. Sometimes it seemed as if someone had deliberately emptied his purse over the trash but, lavish or reckless, the gift served its purpose: after the first few coins had trickled down, Jeth could not bale the load fast enough.

Friday was butchers' day, unanimously regarded as the black spot of the week. Hour after hour the lorries came piled high with all the gore and waste from every butcher in Barnsley. Ernie and I would spend the whole day surrounded by a sea of blood and mangled tissue and dark-stained cardboard, retching at the stench of dried, rotting flesh, slipping down on patches of grease and the stains of body-juices and tormented by swarms of flies driven beserk by the sight of slaughter. Like ghouls we waded waist-high through a welter of stale carnage, wrestling with flapping cartons pasted with blackened entrails, all but overcome by gigantic cardboard slabs seemingly revitalised by the gushing blood, until our clothes, smeared with crimson, reeked of death and our gloves and shoes were stuffed with pigs' lights.

Often on those Friday mornings we arrived to find the first loads piled eight to ten feet high in front of the works entrance. The only way of disposing of the mound was to climb over it to reach the shute. A sheer, granite wall provides less formidable obstacles than those gentle, deceptive slopes. You found a handgrip and the entire side collapsed. Footholds disintegrated under the slightest pressure. We would leap fairly on to its back, scrambling like dogs obsessed with hygiene, and watch in disbelief as the summit soared higher and higher above us and our bodies prostrated themselves on the ground before it. Once we had struggled to the top and stood astride it, its great mouth opened hungrily and tried to swallow us. We sank into a pitch-black, nightmarish world of evil smells where demon fingers prodded and poked remorselessly, to be half-smothered by paper bags and half-strangled by typing ribbon. Inch by inch the mass slipped forward and as it toppled on the edge of the platform Jeth would loudly caution us not to go down with it, not because he valued our safety but because he had instructions to bind only paper and cardboard, and spoilt bales reduced his bonus.

But observation of his warning was never easy when the very ground under our feet shifted erratically, and homicidal forces in the writhing garbage silently thrust us towards the slide and the deep, powerfully surging chant of the great hammer challenged us to throw ourselves before it. Somehow, even life at Pogmoor had something to commend it and so I never surrendered. Ernie went down, however. I remember a particularly large landslide hurtling down the shute when suddenly it grew arms and legs of familiar proportions and began struggling frantically against the uncompromising force of gravity. Immediately Jeth raced to switch off the machine, although he must have known instinctively that he could never reach it in time. The Old Man and I, having nothing better to do, stood by and watched. At first Ernie could make no headway whatsoever, and was at one point only four inches away from becoming adjusted to take a much larger size in shoes. Then, slowly, painfully slowly, he pulled himself up the steep, wooden ramp, worn smooth and polished over the years, until he could reach the pole that I held out to him. After a few moments' indecision as to whether he wanted to join me or me to join him, he was once more sitting in the pile of cardboard on the platform, huffing and blowing, while the press, cheated of its victim, roared in fury and redoubled its attack on the half-finished bale. Finally he squared his cap and looked down the chute.

'Bloody 'Ell!' he said — and he never mentioned the incident again.

That was also the day that Jeth walked into the mess room wearing a hat for the first time. It was a brown-check trilby in the style that had been fashionable a few years earlier, with a small, red feather tucked into a broad, dark-green band. He had perched it low across his forehead, so that his bulbous eyes looked out from either side of the rim and only his long nose and chin saved his face from being completely eclipsed. Tug stared at him stonily.

'Take that daft 'at off,' he ordered. 'Tha looks more like an 'orse than ever.'

'Nay, Ah'm bound to wear it while Ah'm loadin' ' incinerator, or Ah'll set mi' 'air afire.'

The incinerator, marked by a tall, brick chimney, lay beside the path from the mess room down to the press. Once in a while the lorries would bring large quantities of refuse which, in the interests of public health or the good name of the manufacturer had to be destroyed rather than merely tipped. There was a sunken bath about ten feet square immediately in front of the oven, and the only way of crossing it was via a line of very unstable stepping-stones. The water lay brown and stagnant like thick, oily soup and gave off an odour more powerfully evil than I had ever experienced, as though every tramp in Barnsley had washed his socks in it. When the wind unkindly blew the stink across the path, we had to run the gauntlet with our noses pinched to avoid being sick. But Jeth would trip along those stones as if he were fording a mountain stream bubbling in the blossom-scented air of spring, and I thought he must be superhuman until they told me he had lost his sense of smell.

'Can't tha wear a flat cap like everyone else, then?' Tug persisted.

''Course not. Ah keep that for laikin' football. Ah'm not muckyin' that.'

'Who's tha laik for?'

'' Social Club. Ah'm ' first team goalie.'

'Are tha that good?'

'Ah am that.'

'Tha're kiddin' 'im, now,' said Pat. 'Tha were picked 'cos tha're only one as can jump up to ' crossbar.'

'Ow's tha mean? There i'nt a better goalie i' ' league, Ah can tell thi now. If it weren't for me, we'd 'ave been laced o' Saturday.'

''E's only 'avin' thee on, kid,' Pat sneered. ''E couldn't stop a back'eel from a Girl Guide.'

'Tha should 'ave seen mi o' Saturday, then. Ah made some brilliant saves all through ' match. Thee ask our Trevor.'

''Ow many did tha win by?'

'We didn't. We lost fourteen-nowt. But that shows thee what pressure Ah were under. No-one could 'ave saved none on 'em. An' ' ref' were biased. A good dozen o' their goals were offside' 'E only gave 'em 'cos their centre-forward were gie'in' 'im a lift 'ome.'

'Ah don't fancy that bloke's chances,' Pat told us. 'Last time a ref' narked 'im, 'e tried to run 'im down on a pedestrian crossin'. Then 'e'd ' cheek to say 'is brakes 'adn't worked.'

'They 'adn't Ah tell thee. Ah pulled ' 'and-brake aht tryin' to stop ' car. An' Ah got fined for careless, bloody drivin' ... But Ah reckon Ah nicked that bugger all t' same.'

Every few days an articulated lorry would appear to collect the scores of bales that had accumulated in the long, dark stores and take them to the mills to be reduced to pulp again. The proceeds of sale were shared between the Corporation and all the workers involved in collecting salvage, and consequently there was very little waste. More often than not, the lorry crawled away grossly overloaded — its stated capacity was fourteen tons but it had not taken long to establish that sixteen tons did it no apparent harm — even to the extent of fitting a bale across the passenger seat. On average, it took about an hour and a half to load, with two men bringing out the bales, a mechanical shovel lifting them on to the trailer, and then Pat and the driver packing them in neat rows four layers deep, and all the time the hot sun did his level best to set fire to us, and great rivers of sweat poured from us, and the endless manoeuvres of the mechanical shovel drew dust and poisonous fumes into our stifled lungs. Tug and I were normally responsible for the first stage of the operation, taking it in turns to fetch out the bales on a two-wheeled luggage carrier known as '' wheels'. It was a singularly daunting task because the wheels could only carry one bale at a time and the great scoop could accommodate four, so it was necessary to make eight, rapid trips to fill it just once, and matters, far from becoming easier with the passing of time, worsened steadily as we removed the first lines of bales, for the trips became longer and more and more hurried until, when utter exhaustion had brought us to the point of collapse, we were almost sprinting in and out of the store. We fostered a suspicion that the hourly cost of hiring the mechanical shovel was deducted from our salvage bonus, and no man is so much a slave as when his own interest is master. It was a grim business, even with Tug there to throw on three bales to my one, but painful hardship descended into agonizing torture when he and Ernie were elsewhere and the only available assistance was that of the Old Man. Though as strong as a bull, he was lame in one leg, so that the entire onus of bringing out the bales wrapped itself like iron chains around his workmate's limbs. After pushing the wheels for half an hour, time and an end of time had lost all meaning for this wretch, and the blood was roaring through tender veins and filling his head until his skull was bursting through the first membranes of skin, and both feet had been transformed into hard blocks of lead, half-severed at the ankle. His lungs screamed for air and choked immediately as the heavy diesel fumes poured in and dense clouds of dust rasped the windpipe. He emerged to find the bucket like a gaping dragon's mouth lowered to the floor, its steel teeth gouging deep grooves into the earth and creeping menacingly towards his shackled feet. And the Old Man would just stand by the entrance, gazing out at the empty world, and wait.

It was on one of these occasions that I first saw the rats. By now, I had come to disbelieve the stories bandied about by Pat and Jeth of vermin armies roving over the depot, for I had not yet seen so much as a whisker, so I no longer approached every corner expecting to be ambushed by teeming hordes of them. We had cleared about half the contents of the left-hand store with nothing more amiss than a split bale. It was perpetually dark inside, but even so I could make out the form of a black-and-white cat and several kittens settled peacefully at the back on top of the cardboard, and if ever there was an indication that all was well it was that disarming scene. It proved, under the circumstances, then, a trifle disturbing, just as I was slipping the wheels beneath two hundredweight of tightly pressed cardboard, to see a long, black, pointed head, about a foot long silently appear by my side at knee height. In that very instant my entire frame received an emergency supply of liquid oxygen and my stomach wrapped itself around both tonsils. Two red eyes, burning with a terrible, evil fire stared balefully and intensely above a fearsome array of glittering, wicked-looking teeth. Far from Pat and Jeth having indulged in a harmless scaremongering they had clearly not told me half the tale. It was like something out of a horror film. What was most disturbing was that the monster plainly did not live on a diet of cardboard scraps and he looked peckish. I glanced at the cat thinking to set her on it, but no; probably her first sight of this creature had induced a virgin-birth. Should I offer the cat instead ... ?

A faint, characteristic, doggy tang seemed to revive my breathing system and to suggest an explanation rational enough for me to open my eyes again. This was Mack, Jeth's dog, which Pat had mentioned to Tug and me on our first day here. There never was a stranger looking animal: he could have traced his ancestry to every breed of dog that ever existed. Jeth maintained that he was the son of an Alsatian bitch and an arrogant, if not resourceful, corgi, but he was jet-black from nose to tail with a smooth coat that rippled like silk, a head somewhere between that of a greyhound and an English collie, and the build of a doberman. Not even his mother could have persuaded herself that he was showdog material, and it scarcely enhanced his appearance to have had almost his entire upper lip chewed away so that his teeth and gums were laid bare in a mute snarl. Nonetheless, he was hailed as being worth his weight in lead scrap, for he derived immense satisfaction from slaughtering colonies of rats, and would volunteer for long periods of duty and go without his meals just for the pleasure of sinking his fangs into vermin flesh. As soon as he saw the lorry from the paper mills turning into the depot he would slink across the tip, drenching his wake with saliva, and slip into the store, there to wait patiently like a macabre embodiment of Death. And few of his victims escaped the consequences of that vision.

He offered no greeting, and I, realizing that this was not a social call, made no advance either, but continued to take out the bales, one by one, working further and further into the gloom until the

only contacts with the outside world were the alternate roaring and
purring of the mechanical shovel and the echoing sounds of the Old
Man spitting just beyond the entrance. Each time I levered a bale
on to the wheels and pulled it away Mack would be pressed against
the next row with his nose to the ground, sniffing excitedly and
fidgeting with nervous energy, impatient to dart into the yawning
cavity. Sometimes he was more than usually eager and I heard him
yelp once or twice as though the wheels had nipped him, and he
emerged with a fresh wound on his ragged muzzle and dark streams
of blood trickling down his gums. But on each occasion there was
no trace of life on the ground behind the bale, and then he would
turn his head and glower at me, to my growing discomfort, as if it
were all my fault and he would not tolerate any further obstruction.

He continued to act like this down to the very last line of bales,
and though I now understood his purpose the lack of success
clearly showed that he was being over enthusiastic. Even so it was
with great relief that I drew out the end bale from that last line. His
very behaviour gave cause for alarm, and I was, frankly, thankful
that he was disappointed.

A writhing knot of rats squealed and chattered in an alcove in the
back wall. It was so unexpected that I completely froze in an
untimely paralysis. They appeared in no way infatuated with me
either, and spared me no embarrassment in their haste to get away.
In one mad rush they flew through the gaping breach, scrambling
over the wheels and my shoes, and scratching across the trouser legs
of my overalls. It was like being bombarded with spiked cricket
balls, and done so quickly that I was still motionless when they
were streaking across the open floor.

But Mack was quicker. Two bodies were settling in death at my
feet even before I looked down, and he was charging after the rest
like one possessed. A more efficient killer than that black mongrel
never walked this earth. Without checking his stride, he would seize
his fleeing quarry nicely at the back of the neck, throw up his head
and toss a mass of brown, lifeless fur through the air while chasing
the next. Death seemed to be to him a drug to which he was
helplessly addicted, and as his jaws closed on his prey he
experienced a moment's bliss which aggravated the lust to taste its
awfulness just once more. Not one escaped alive. We surveyed the
grim aftermath when Jeth returned to his capacity as undertaker

with a bucket and a long skewer. Twelve bodies were strewn across the floor, all full-grown rats and not a mark on one of them. And, his business finished, Mack had disappeared.

After that I saw rats in their scores. It was difficult to see how I could have failed to notice them. They were everywhere, on the tip, in the stores and behind the press, in the mounds of cardboard that Ernie and I shepherded down the chute. They scuttled daily across the mess room floor, and took up lodgings in the cupboards. The whole site was riddled with rat holes. They had even burrowed into the leather armchair which was the Old Man's favourite seat.

It was common practice for those who brought packed meals to keep them on the table, securely fastened in tin boxes, for those who did not soon learned that the rats levied a heavy tax on everything not dressed with mustard. Yet, surprisingly, only Tug and I made a point of eating out. On Mondays, Wednesdays and Thursdays we joined the queue outside the fish-and-chip shop in Cresswell Street, drawn to savour again the chef's speciality, an exquisitely flavoured fish rissole. The rest of the week found us at the corner ship buying corned beef sandwiches for one shilling and sixpence each, or ham rolls at two shillings on days when we felt inclined to be lavish. Afterwards, rain or shine, we finished at the working men's club on Pogmoor Road to wash away the stale tastes of the depot that lingered on our tonsils. It was a quiet crowd, friendly but reserved, which collected there to discuss the day's affairs or watch the last few overs before lunch on the television behind the bar. There was a man with a fascinating nervous condition that threw his body into violent contortions every half-minute or so which he accompanied with a few syllables of gibberish. Nobody minded provided he restrained himself from doing it at a time likely to put the English batsmen off their stroke. A retired collier from Winter Terrace was almost a fixture there, and none more welcome, although there were muttered misgivings about his pet chihuahua which looked upon the plastic seat covering on the side benches as some kind of elevated lavatory. Most of the mid-day customers came from the factory on the other side of West Road, and these we never saw from one lunchtime to the next, but there frequently joined the company a small, squat man, who fed sixpences into the 'one-armed bandit' machine as though it were dying of malnutrition, and whom I had often observed pushing a delapidated, wooden cart down to the shed where Pat bailed newspapers and booklets. It did not take long for Tug to discover that Pat was sorting out all the girlie magazines from the paper salvage and selling them by the barrowload to this strange individual. At first, we were told that he hawked them round the hostels and old folk's homes, but Tug later heard that he owned a fish-and-chip shop somewhere and was anxious to maintain the roaring trade that had developed within days of his first wandering down to the depot.

We had only gone to the club originally because Randy Steve had taken us there one Wednesday. He was a road-sweeper in that area and they could always rely on him sweeping their streets up the hill on a Wednesday because that was the day on which he committed adultery with a lady on the estate. We all knew her, and you could tell by the gleam in her eye every time she saw a dustman that his visit was the highlight of her week, but to Steve it was just all in a day's work. In fact, that was the reason why he could only spare her the Wednesday morning, for he was fully booked every other day on similar engagements all over town. Just to look at him you would wonder what on earth the attraction was, and no doubt he too was staggered by it all, for he was a very quiet, unassuming sort. But matters had got to such a pitch that what had begun as a polite response to a few maidens' prayers had turned into a regular service for damsels in distress — and sometimes their mothers too — and he had been forced to arrange his cleaning rounds to fit in with his rota. The streets he visited might not be very clean when he left, but apparently there was many a grateful housewife to wave him off. His sexual prowess had made him a legend in his own lifetime — he was said to have sired a quarter of the intake at one infants' school — and men admired him as much as the women. I only ever met him at Pogmoor or first thing in the morning down at the yard, for you could rarely catch him outside during the day. He used to hide his barrow in the salvage depot while he attended his Wednesday appointments, and then he would be away two hours at a stretch. But he always went up for a drink afterwards, for the girl at Pogmoor, he said, was thirsty work.

Tug was always hesitant about walking into the club, and once there, never drank more than half a pint, which was odd in a man whose notion of heaven on earth was to have his domestic water system connected to unlimited supplies of draught bitter. One day, after he had refused, as always, a second glass, I pointed out this mild hypocrisy.

'Nay, Ah can't afford to, nip,' he said, and his face rapidly filling with scarlet. 'To tell thee ' truth, Ah can't afford 'afe a pint on its own.'

'It's only a shilling a glass.'

'Arr. An' a shillin' a day's five shillin' a week; an' two shillin' a day's ten bob a week. What wi' all mi stoppages Ah've only eleven pound odd at ' bottom o' ' note. That's bahn to 'ave to see Maureen an' ' kids through ' week, soon, an' all. Fact is, Ah think fish an' chips every day's goin' above mi means.'

'But you can't live on fresh air — even if you could find any round here.'

'Ah'll 'ave to bring sandwiches, and eat in that pig 'ole. Tha sees, wi' mi comin' in 'ere, Ah've not been able to take 'er aht at ' weekend.'

Shortly afterwards, Tug started to bring a large flask and a wad of sandwiches consisting of at least half a loaf. I looked back to that first day when we were out sweeping the roads, and remembered how he had gone into the pub looking as radiant as a leper in an all-in wrestling match. With clearer hindsight, I saw the anxieties that tightened his jaws momentarily as he stood at the bar, and the pangs of guilt that dulled his moistening eyes. How true it is that a rich man's pleasure is a poor man's sin.

'It's Poggy for thee.'

Those words keep coming to torment me. I can hear the sneering whine in Stan's voice even now, and sometimes in my dreams I go walking down the stony road and wander unwillingly through the silent desolation of that God-forsaken place. It is always the same, the stench, the piles of spewed-up litter, the rusty, iron sheeting, the shabby, brick buildings sinking into the sprawling, dusty wastes. I am there still, for no-one, once tainted with its awful squalor, can ever escape. It seems to be everywhere, its stagnant breath clinging to me like a cloak and staining even the darkness with its shadow, an ugly grave for the hopes of the men brought there to rot in filth, disease and all things vile. When I was young they told me there was only misery and despair at the end of the world and I believed them. Those terrors are like rain on the desert sands to me now, for I have seen it.

5 The Cleanest Road

Not five minutes' walk from the town centre and you stroll, with perhaps unashamed surprise, into one of the pleasanter areas of Barnsley. Up Market Hill, past that imposing piece of architecture, the Town Hall, that anywhere else might have inspired whole galleries of paintings and volumes of poetry, but which seemed here to be used by the local artists only to check their watches, along Church Street with St Mary's on one side in her poor, black robes and the polished brass plates of prosperous solicitors on the other. And there you are, on the edge of an urban oasis. The Miners' Memorial stands stiffly by the cross roads like a towering border guard, and you look across at the green, the greener green, of lines of majestic trees which grace the passage of Huddersfield Road, until dark greenness eats into your very soul. Everything is different. The road you must cross to get there runs down the hill like a river between barren scrub and lush grassland. Beyond it great Victorian houses with huge empty windows retire behind the veils of dense privet hedges and rhododendrons thick with spiders' webs. Shady avenues branching out from Huddersfield Road appease the eye made sore by a harsh landscape of stone, brick, iron and concrete. Slipping gently into decay, it lives on in faded elegance, like an old recluse oblivious to the changes of the modern world, dreaming only of the golden days of a bygone age, and filled with imperishable dignity. Town planners and estate agents describe it by that curious term 'residential', as though 'people' do not live in other parts of the town. Some of the larger houses have been converted into offices, others into surgeries for dentists and doctors. One or two prominent members of the Labour Party have settled there, possibly as a spearhead for social equality, but to this day it has remained true to what it always was, the last, crumbling link with an old-world gentility.

By tacit and kind permission of the owner, Sid and his road-sweeping crew settled down to their snap every day in the garage in front of a tall, stone house on Huddersfield Road — tacit in the sense that they understood consent would instantly have been granted if anyone had come down to ask what the hell they thought they were doing there. It was a roomy garage, well appointed, with large crates and empty paraffin cans to represent armchairs and a small square of oily carpet laid beneath the window. The cart, a battery-operated hand-cart, was always drawn up inside the entrance and the garage door closed for, as Sid would say, out of sight, out of mind.

'That's ' only trouble,' Sid explained, as he pulled the door down. 'Nice day like this an' we're forced to shut ussens in. Not reight.'

'Arr,' said Willie.

Willie was far from us, however. He was absorbed in Sid's copy of the *Daily Mirror*, which he read, from the first to the last page, in less than a minute. Not yet thirty, he had the complexion and constitution of a pink blancmange. Tides of fat ebbed and flowed across his great moonface whenever he turned his head, and all that ever lay still were his gentle, blue eyes that stared apologetically through thick, tortoiseshell-rimmed spectacles.

'Where's Lampy?' asked Willie.

'Ah told thee. Fox wants to see 'im 'cos 'e skived off yesterday.'

'Oh, arr.'

Apparently inspired by the moment, Willie walked over to me and insisted on shaking hands. It was the third time we had done so in the past hour but he seemed to feel much better for it, for he went back quietly enough to his seat afterwards.

'Who's Fox?' I asked.

Sid did not appear to have heard me at first. He was standing on a crate, rummaging through a cupboard high on the wall to bring, from behind grimy bottles of turpentine and jars of grease, a bag of sugar and a tin, marked 'nails', containing tea leaves. Not for him that stewed concoction which comes out of a flask. There was nothing that so sustained Sid in performing his daily duties as a mug of freshly brewed tea in the early morning, and he had used considerable ingenuity to devise means of obtaining it. Every so often he brought a small bottle of paraffin to refuel the primus stove that he had found lying in the corner of the garage. There was a cold water tap in the end wall, and he kept the kettle hidden under the floorboards. The three of them took it in turns to supply the tea and sugar, and Willie, who was the only one who took milk, brought about a fluid ounce of it in an old aspirin bottle. The crockery was packed neatly in the well of the cupboard top, and the only person likely to find them would actually have been looking for the headlamp from his 1930 Morris Oxford.

''E's ' Superintendent.'

'I didn't know his name was Fox.'

''E don't neither. That's just what we call 'im. Tha sees, 'is men are foxes, allus laikin' an' gettin' 'idded so as no-one can see 'em. So, 'e 'as to be a Fox an' all, craftier than 'is men. 'E stands in shopways an' be'ind trees spyin' on thee, an' when 'e sees thee slackin', 'e jumps aht on thee.'

'Arr.'

'What do people think when they see the entire Cleansing Department playing hide and seek all over Barnsley?'

'Ah don't know. We 'a'nt 'ad it so bad though, not since 'e were watchin' us at ' back o' a 'edge in a garden up Granville Street, an' missis there reported 'im 'cos she thowt 'e were pissin' be'ind it.'

''E got Lampy, though,' Willie remarked.

'Ah, but 'e'll 'ave to watch what 'e says wi' Lampy, or 'e'll get brayed.'

'Why?' I asked.

'Don't tha know Lampy?' Sid asked.

'No.'

''E were born i' Park Road, afore they knocked it down. Worst area i' Barnsley, it were. Allus feightin' they were, women an' all. Tha'd get beat up just for walkin' ovver their bit o' pavement. Ah shouldn't argue wi' someone from Park Road anyway. An' Lampy's good wi' 'is fists, Ah can tell thee. 'E'd 'ave thee on thi back afore tha'd disagreed wi' 'im.'

The sound of heavy footsteps coming up the drive interrupted this disquieting social survey.

'That's 'im,' said Sid. 'Gie 'im a 'and wi' t' door, kid; it sticks.'

Appearances may be deceptive, but there must be limits. The terror of Barnsley was tall, skinny, acutely asthmatic, and the nearest he came to produce bulging muscles was to get a ruck in his jacket sleeve. On top of that he was partially deaf and complained of rheumatism in his lower spine. But Sid gave me a warning nod and a look that said 'I told you so'.

'What's 'e said to thee?'

''E said Ah were too good for this job, an' 'e'd see to it that Ah were ' next Lord Mayor.'

'That should be nice,' said Willie, approvingly.

''E's off badly, so Mike told mi to bugger off,' he finally confessed, helping himself to tea. 'Where's that spoon?'

He picked it up from Willie's knee. Willie, who had been absent-mindedly picking his nose and rolling the extracts into tiny balls in their one and only spoon, watched in wide-eyed horror as the Park Road Basher stirred them vigorously into his tea.

'It's not reight,' continued Lampy. 'Ah take 'afe an hour off an' they lace into me. 'E's off for a whole day an' nowt's said. Tha knows, there's one law for ' rich an' one for ' poor.'

'Why don't tha go to ' Union?' said Sid.

'Nay, they're worse than ' Tories. At least ' Tories pay thee, an' not ' other way round. An' where's it got us, Ah ask thee? We're still ' worse paid men i' ' country.'

'Arr.'

'Sithee. Ah said to 'Arry, last week, as we should come aht on strike. 'E says "Executive's decided against it". Now where's ' sense i' me payin' folk to tell me Ah can't do what Ah want?'

'Tha can't do nowt baht ' Union, though.'

'Tha can't do nowt wi' ' em, tha means. 'Afe on 'em, as soon as they're elected, are makin' piles for theirsens as fast as they can, an' arse'ole to ' rest on us. They're supposed to be gettin' rid o' capitalism, not takin' it ovver. It's these buggers 'ere in their big 'ouses as they should be after, them who's worked us to death, an' lived on ' fat o' ' land.'

He surveyed the rippling lake of long grass leading up to the house and sniffed at the sun-blistered paint on the gable end.

'Get rid on 'em, Ah say.'

'Where would tha put 'em?'

'Where ' rest on us 'as 'ad to live. Let 'em taste a bit o' their own medicine. We should all be livin' i' places like these. Willie should 'ave this 'ouse, shouldn't tha, Willie?'

'Ah don't know as Ah could do wi' all this 'ere garden,' Willie replied. 'It's an awful lot o' diggin.'

'Ah, but wi' all this garden, tha could dig just as much as tha wanted. Tha could plant all them roses tha said tha'd bowt.'

'Ah don't think as Ah'm good at growin' roses, though.'

''Ow's tha mean? Ah told thee to put thi tea leaves round ' base when tha's finished suppin'. 'A'nt tha been feedin' ' em?'

'Oh, arr. Ah did just like tha said. An' Ah've even gied 'em tea when Ah've not 'ad none missen. But they've all died. Ah reckon it scalds 'em.'

Every day, between half-past eight and nine o'clock, we trudged along the gutters of Huddersfield Road pulled along by our sturdy brushes, swinging before us with long, sleepy sighs. It was hard work, and this and the tension produced by every passing lorry driver testing by how few tenths of an inch he could avoid hitting us brought us frequently to a halt and a moment's rest against a garden wall. Purely by coincidence, there was always at this time a steady procession of young girls, slowly wending their way up the road to the Barnsley High School For Girls at the top of the rise, hundreds of girls in groups of twos and threes as far as the eye could see, girls with billowing, summer skirts coming barely halfway down their thighs carelessly displaying their shapely form; girls radiant with the flush of youth, in that fleeting, supreme bloom of their spring, haughty, sensual, vain, the wakening flower of womanhood revealing all its delicate perfection beneath the sparkling jewels of the dew.

'There's some nice stuff there an' reight,' said Sid, appreciately, nodding across at this endless parade. 'An' Ah bet it's all goin' spare. They're all there, nip, just waitin' on thee an' young Willie 'ere. Go on, man, while tha's chance.'

Willie nodded in agreement and continued to watch them pass. Beside him, Lampy looked on with only half an eye in a very detached fashion, totally becoming to the true idealist. Sid shook his head, sadly.

'Tha're wastin' thissens, tha two. Can't tha see, they're all askin' for it: randy as 'ell they are at that age. Ee, if Ah were only twenty year younger ...'

''Ow far did tha get wi' their mothers, then?'

'Nay, it were different, then: women didn't go around showin' all they'd got, then. 'Course, we 'ad our ways an' means, though, o' findin' aht. An' once we knew, there were no stoppin' us. Oh, arr, we 'ad it 'undreds o' times.'

In our various ways we watched them come and go, four drowsy figures, unshaven, unkempt and in dusty overalls sitting under the shadows on a low, stone wall with the stubble of former iron railings on the top adding to the difficulty. And they passed us by as though we were not even there. Not once that flash from the eye corner by which Woman reassures herself she has ensnared the gaze of the man she coldly ignores. Road-sweepers are not the most romantic of heroes nor the most fashionable lovers. Even the occasional 'Oi oi!' from Sid failed to overcome their maidenly shyness or to gain a single glance not spiked with contempt.

'Ee, just look at 'em.'

'Arr. Ah am. But tha 'ad thi turn twenty year sin', so tha're not sharin' wi' us.'

'Thi turn's nivver o'er. 'Sides, they weren't as advanced when Ah were young as they are today. Bloody born wi' bras on these days.'

'Tha're reight. Ah wish they'd sent me to college, now. Ah shouldn't waste mi time studyin'.'

'You would if they did.'

'Tha can't kid me abaht college, nip. They're sex mad, these college girls — especially them as went to an all-girls school. It's reight enough! They get reight sex-starved i' them places, and wi no men abaht, like, so by ' time they leave to go to college they're goin' bonkers for a feller: they can't get enough on it. Ah know all abaht it, nip. My mate were a caretaker at one on them schools, an' 'e told me. 'E showed mi what they wrote on ' bog doors an' all. It's ' worst stuff Ah've ever read, enough to make thee sick. They know far more abaht it than we do, tha knows.'

'Tell us what some on 'em said, Sid,' pleaded Willie.

'Ah can't remember it now. Ah know as 'e were 'avin' it off wi' abaht every girl i' ' school though. 'E just did it wi' one, an' ' rest threatened to tell on 'im 'cos she were under age. 'E 'ad every girl from thirteen to eighteen comin' to 'im. Damn near broke 'is 'ealth.'

'Would 'e let us into ' bogs to 'ave a read?'

'Nay. Their 'eadmistress caught 'im at it be'ind ' boilers wi' two on 'em. They put 'im i' prison for it. Ah were fair disgusted when

Ah 'eard what 'e'd gone in for.'

'I should imagine most people would find it a little disturbing.'

'Exactly. Damned old cow, she were. Ah bet she only told on 'im 'cos 'e wouldn't do it to 'er.'

The latter part of the morning would find us anywhere on that hillside, taken wherever the winds of fancy blew us, sometimes in a garage, sometimes lying low in a piece of secluded waste land, sometimes measuring the flow of traffic from a shady, garden wall and, not infrequently, sweeping the streets. If we saw the inspector's van prowling around we would instantly be out in the road in a flurry of brushes. There were times when we would comes across Randy Steve's barrow poking out from behind a garden wall, and Sid in a voice that had never quite mastered the delicate art of whispering would announce to the whole neighbourhood that he was 'knockin' all 'Ell aht o' 'er at Number Six again'. But more days than not we would never see a soul we knew. Slowly, we drifted through those sleepy, surburban backwaters, Willie and I gouging out time-hardened sediment from the gutters with round-headed brooms, while Lampy coaxed dust from the pavement by long, easy strokes using a broad, soft-bristled brush. Usually, Willie and I worked on opposite sides of the street, so that Sid, who shovelled the piles we made into the cart which trailed behind him like a tame, red cow, meandered erratically down the road like a drunkard trying to walk along both pavements at once.

'Tha're too slow to catch cold, nip,' commented Sid, leaning on his shovel beside me as I rounded up on to the heap a few flecks of earth. 'Tha're not siftin' for gold, tha knows. We'll all get paid at ' end o' ' week just t' same whether we leave all ' muck 'ere or scrub t' street down wi' Vim.'

'What's that young lad laikin' at up there?' shouted Lampy at the end of the street. 'Is 'e settin' plants in?'

'Look where them two are now,' Sid pointed out. 'Ah'll be 'afe way through mi dinner time afore Ah catch up wi' 'em 'cos o' thee. Tha's only need to take ' topsoil off, an' what don't get done gets left. Choose 'ow, it'll be just as mucky tomorrow.'

'Tha're tryin' too 'ard,' said Willie, coming back to inspect the progress and shaking hands. 'Tha'll nivver get nowhere doin' that. Sithee, just watch me an' tha'll learn summat.'

He swung his broom into the gutter and pressed the butt of the handle against his ample stomach. About a foot of the shaft immediately disappeared, apparently swallowed by his innards with no obvious ill-effects. Leaning lightly upon it he followed it slowly down the street gently rocking the broom head by deft muscular action in his wrists and abdomen.

'Easy, i'nt it?' he called back.

I nodded. He continued down the street at a steady pace, yet with a leisureliness that almost amounted to indifference, and the mound of litter and grit churning before him swelled with every stroke he made. After about ten yards he arrived at the grate of a drain, and with a few brisk movements sent a torrent of earth and rubble plunging into the bubbling, hissing blackness below.

'That's 'ow it's done, nip,' Willie explained. 'That way, tha does what tha're told, tha gets a rest at t' same time, an' when there's a drain 'andy, Sid gets one an' all.'

It was a refreshingly simple lesson, and in scarcely the time it takes to pick up a broom handle I had acquired the finer skills of road-sweeping and was now able to keep abreast with the rest of them. But, only five minutes later, as I was about to discharge a large quantity of silt into the sewer, Sid charged up from behind me and knocked the broom clean out of my grasp.

'Not now, kid,' he rasped, 'An' look normal. There's ' gulley wagon 'ere.'

Consciously looking normal must be a feat verging on the impossible, and is not made any easier by the suggestion that what you have always taken for granted as being normal is clearly not good enough. You suddenly realize that your arms are like steel rods against your sides and so you swing them from side to side and round and round in a casual sort of fashion. Your right leg is, unbeknown to you till now, three inches shorter than your left, and the only way of disguising the fact is to hold one of them out in front of you or wrap it around the other. Worst of all you are not relaxed because you are not whistling, so you whistle, vainly chasing up and down the scale for the opening note of that well-known song you are whistling, and your eyes flash about the heavens and the earth because it helps you to whistle. By the time the gulley wagon was upon us I was looking about as normal as a five-legged horse. Sid saluted the occupants as it passed with a touch of his cap, and they cheerfully waved in return. We watched the lorry receding into the distance, its long suction pipe tapping insistently against the tank on its back.

'If tha're bahn to put ' muck down t' drain, make sure they're not watchin' thee, first. It's them as 'as to get it all up again. Cussin' an' swearin' they are every time they come. Tha'll 'ear 'em tell thee it mun rain porridge 'ere, but don't thee let on, 'cos if they catch thee at it, they'll 'ave thee up that 'ose an' gone for good.'

It was always Lampy who broke the news that it was dinner time, not because he had any special authority to do so, but because he was the only one with a reliable watch. Sid kept a pocket watch in his jacket, but it only seemed to work when he shook it. There was a running dispute between them and the Superintendent as to precisely when they could stop work, and when they had to start again, and it had been going on for years. It was common ground that they had from twelve until one o'clock to eat their dinners, but as Lampy argued almost every day, this was only sensible in their case if they added a period of walking time on to either side. None of them lived on that side of town, so that if at twelve o'clock they were somewhere in Wilthorpe on the borough boundary, they would arrive back home or at the depot with just enough time left to get back for one. This was obviously absurd, so at one time they used to finish each morning at half-past-eleven and walk back into town, but then the Superintendent found out and threatened them with the sack if they left off sweeping before the stroke of twelve. As a counter-measure they took to sweeping back along Huddersfield Road towards the town centre during the last hour of the morning, so that at noon they were able to set out for lunch from exactly the same position as in the past. The real winners in this conflict, however, were neither the sweepers nor the Superintendent, but the residents on Huddersfield Road. For the payment of a modest sum in the form of rates they had the road swept three times a day, before nine, before noon and in the middle of the afternoon as the crew carried out a similar routine to clock-off as early as possible. It was beyond doubt the cleanest road in the borough, and businessmen and town-councillors were known to direct their chauffeurs miles out of their way to drive along it as a pleasing introduction to visiting clients and industrialists, for whom the name of Barnsley conjured up a large slack heap swarming with people black to the eyeballs in coal dust and saying 'Ee, ba gum' to each other. There cannot be many townships whose future development owed so much to a road-sweeper's claim to an extra half-hour for dinner.

Dustmen, of course, could not eat just anywhere they pleased. They were not actually banned as such from certain establishments but I discovered it was a fact of life when I walked into one of Barnsley's more expensive hotels one day in a donkey jacket and overalls. It was not merely the icy stare from every customer in the bar lounge which brought this home to me. That might well have been natural reserve. Perhaps the barmaid always greeted her regulars with that rather flat, 'What do you want?' But the way she followed me with a carpet sweeper as I went out left me in no doubt as to the depth of their welcome. Consequently, we enjoyed a rather more limited diet than the average. At the café on Wellington Street you could take away bacon sandwiches or a Cornish pasty; at the restaurant at the bottom of the arcade there was always pie and peas. But most of us in the Cleansing Department relied exclusively on the scores of fish-and-chip shops around Barnsley, and the only way to provide variety for the palate was to visit them in turn. We all had our particular favourites. One of the most popular was the little shop in the dingy Gas Nook. Some sweepers would even go as far as the place at Town End on a fine day. The best-qualified person to consult if you wanted to try something different was Norman the yardman. He was the unrivalled authority on all aspects of local fish-and-chippery; even more amazing, he was able to identify the place where a man had bought his dinner by eating just one chip, and though he often made mistakes he lived by them and at no great expense. The rest of us regarded his abilities as being nothing short of miraculous, so that a dinner hour without a tale about Norman's prowess being aired around the canteen — and no-one could tell a better story than Norman — was like a meal without salt.

One afternoon we acquired an honorary addition to the crew in the form of a large black-and-white dog. Willie had thrown it the remnants of his tomato sandwich when we first saw it earlier that day, and the animal clearly thought it was eating its membership card. It wore no collar, its coat was matted and it was evidently a stray, but it sat on the wall with the rest of us as good as gold, cocking its head with polite attention as Sid and Lampy talked, and wagging its tail whenever we laughed. Once or twice Willie murmured something about taking it home.

'Mind, we 'ad this trouble afore Fox came,' Lampy was saying, brooding over the dinner problem again. 'They're all t' same, once they're in a position to shove their men about. It goes to their 'eads. Look at 'im who was there afore Fox.'

'Ah don't remember 'im,' said Willie.

'Tha weren't 'ere, then,' said Lampy. 'Now, 'e wouldn't even let thee 'ave a piss.'

''E couldn't stop thee. That's natural, that is.'

'Couldn't 'e? 'E once caught one o' 'is men goin' down ' bogs i' Peel Square, an' 'e says, "Where're tha bahn?" so 'e says, "To ' toilet," an' does tha know what 'e says? 'E says, "Tha does them things afore tha comes to work, an' not durin'." So ' bloke says, "If Ah can't go to ' toilet now, Ah'll do it i' gutter, so tha's a choice." An' 'e were sacked on t' spot.'

'Ah should think 'e were pleased, an' all,' said Willie giggling, ''E could to ' bog, then.'

'Arr, per'aps. Tha wouldn't 'ave got me down Peel Square bogs i' them days, though,' said Sid. 'Not even if Ah were bustin'.'

'Nay, we all 'ave to go,' said Willie, still giggling.

'Arr, but they were them old earth closets, then. Worst i' Barnsley, they were, an' all. Used to stink terrible, didn't they, Lampy? Does tha know, on Saturday neets tha could smell 'em reight up to Town End. Folks would come aht o' ' pubs an' straight down to Peel Square to get rid o' their ale. Floor used to be swimmin' i' sick an' piss ... 'Afe on 'em couldn't aim by then, o' course.'

'Terrible,' Lampy confirmed. 'Tha'd to watch where tha put thi feet an' all, or tha'd be ovver an' drownin' in it.'

'Urrh,' said Willie, his great, round face wrinkled with distaste. 'Ah wouldn't 'ave liked to 'ave been 'im who 'ad to clean it all up.'

'It 'ad to be done, though. They used to 'ave a cart, an' they'd open a little 'atchway at ' back o' ' bog, an' scoop it all out into ' cart. Shit wallopers, we used to call 'em.'

We collapsed in fits of laughter. Willie fell off the wall and laughed on the pavement, while the dog wagged its tail in applause.

'Arr, shit wallopers, 'cos they walloped shit,' said Sid, seeming pleased with himself. 'They opened 'atch, an' got 'old o' ' shit an' walloped it into ' cart.'

Our mirth redoubled.

'They 'ad to work at neet, 'cos no-one would go near 'em i' day. Tha'd just see 'em goin' aht o' ' yard as we were comin' in. Covered in it, they were, an' everyone were 'olding their nose till they'd gone past. An' when folks saw 'em they'd shout "Aye, Aye! It's shit wallopers!" '

Our progress was very slow that afternoon. The sultry weather robbed us of all energy and purpose. Lampy hardly said a word. Sid all but crawled in our wake, frequently breaking the peace of the breathless air to call to us, 'shit wallopers, 'cos they walloped shit,' followed by a hoarse cackle. The dog was not making his job any easier for him as it had dismantled most of the heaps of dust we had swept together long before he arrived with his shovel. Only the dog seemed to have any life at all.

'How are you supposed to work in heat like this?' I said.

'Like every other day i' ' year,' said Lampy. 'Tha don't know tha're born, yet, nip. Tha should be 'ere i' wintertime when thi 'ands are so cold tha thinks thi fingers 'ave come off i' thi gloves. Or what about these trees 'ere in autumn. Worst patch i' Barnsley, this. Only us silly buggers'll do it. When tha gets 'ere first thing, tha can't even see ' pavement for leaves. So tha sweeps 'em all up for about five yards. Then ' wind blows, an' tha looks round, an' there's 'afe a bloody treeful where tha's just been. Then, ' i'spector comes along an' plays 'Ell wi thee for laikin'.'

'Ah wonder where all them leaves come from?' said Willie.

Nobody answered.

'Ah mean, they all fall off one year, an' there's nowt left there. An' next year they're all back again. "Ow's it come abaht? Ah mean, if tha sawed reight down a branch, would tha see all ' leaves waitin' to come up?'

Still nobody answered, although Lampy coughed.

'Tha're a college lad. Tha knows abaht these things, don't tha?'

'I can't answer that.'

'Ah thowt they'd 'ave learnt thee all abaht it there. Them college lads seem to know owt. 'As tha ever seen "University Challenge" on tele?'

'Occasionally.'

He pushed his hand forward and shook mine.

'They know some stuff, tha knows. They're tellin' 'im ' answers, an' Ah don't even understand ' questions ... 'as tha ever been on?'

'No.'

'Tell thee what, then. Ah'll ask thee some questions an' we'll see 'ow many tha gets reight ... What's ' capital o' London?'

'It hasn't got one; how can it?'

'It 'as. New York!'

'But they're both cities.'

He looked straight at me for a few moments, thoroughly puzzled, his blue eyes alive with thought.

'Tha're reight,' he said, after due consideration, and shook hands. 'Ah'll ask thee another one, then: a 'ard one ... What's ' fastest animal i' world?'

'A cheetah.'

'A what?'

'Cheetah!'

That same expression set upon his features, like a teacher trying to understand the strained logic of his pupil.

'Tha're reight. Ah told thee it'd be a 'ard one ... Mind a 'orse's pretty fast an' all.'

'Shit wallopers,' Sid reminded us, "cos they walloped shit.'

'Reight,' said Willie. 'An easy one now. Who's ' richest tart i' world?'

'I can't, in conscience, say I know her.'

'Does tha give in?'

'Yes, but clearly not as often as she has.'

'Queen of America. Tha's got one wrong.'

'I'll admit I'd have been a long time in getting it right. Why a tart, though?'

"Cos she is. They all are.'

'They?'

'Them! Women! All women are tarts, aren't they?'

'I suppose it's one approach. You can always hope.'

Questions and answers chased each other along the street as we walked up the hill and across the ridge, leaving our brooms to trail like snails behind us. Nothing moved in the surrounding silence, either on the land or in the sky, but the stifling air burned our cheeks and the distance was lost in the searing heat. We crossed over into Granville Street and were just settling down on a broad-backed, brick wall when a loud bark reproached us from round the corner for having disappeared without warning. There was a squeal of brakes, a dull thud followed by a yelp of sheer terror. An awful stillness spread across the hill like a heavy smothering sheet. We looked at one another knowing and yet disbelieving, and paralysed by doing both. Suddenly, Sid leapt to his feet and, grasping the handle of his cart, started off smartly down the hill.

'Where're tha off?' yelled Lampy.

'Aht o' ' road. They'll be wantin' a barrow to throw 'im in an' some other silly bugger to do ' throwin'. Are tha comin'?'

The three of us sat for a few moments, locked in thought and measured his reasoning against the call of duty, the morality of doing the decent thing and the beckoning, noble spark of humanity.

Then, we all ran after Sid.

6 Binning

It promised to be a hot day. Archie had said so at least half-a-dozen times in the past twenty minutes. The air was oppressively close and the housing estate seemed deserted except for a few women hanging out the washing before going to work. We tramped slowly down the street behind the dustbin lorry which was gorging itself on the week's refuse from an endless stream of dustbins. Horrible digestive noises erupted from within the vehicle as a mechanical ram continually swept garbage from the rear cavity and forced it deep into its vast stomach. We could hardly make ourselves heard.

'Ah can't reckon it up,' said Archie, after studying the linen at Number Forty-Three. 'Some o' these women mun 'ave 'afe a dozen arses. They go through more knickers in a week than Ah 'ave 'ot dinners. An' look at ' size o' 'ers! She's all arse!'

'It's their pride, i'nt it,' said Bill. 'Ee, Ah'll nivver forget mi sister's face when she fun aht she'd 'ung a pair aht as weren't 'ers. She wouldn't speak to 'im for six month after.'

'Nay, that's a bit 'ard on 'im. We all like a bit on t' side when it's 'andy.'

'Arr, but she weren't mad 'cos of 'is fancy woman. What she minded were that all 'er neighbours could see they were a different size.'

We turned into the next street. At the far end Laughing Gus had already brought out several dustbins on to the pavement and was steadily working his way down towards us.

'Watch thissen when tha lifts this one 'ere up,' he shouted. 'They've dropped their lavatory in it. It's them Poles, tha knows. Shall Ah tell 'em we just pull ' chain i' this country?'

'No sense o' shame, that lad,' muttered Archie. 'Thee come wi' me, nip.'

He scooted down a grass-choked path and round the corner of

the house. I followed him down and then went through a gap in the fence. The house next door appeared to have no dustbin. I looked all over the back garden without success. There was nothing unusual about its absence. Some people seemed ashamed to admit they possessed one. It might be hidden discreetly behind the hedge, in the coal bunker or pushed on to the adjacent premises. One old lady even kept hers in the hall. In the end, a man in a dirty vest, who had been eyeing me suspiciously from the bedroom window, pointed me to the greenhouse, and sure enough it was there, cosily sitting between two tomato plants.

'What's tha carrying' it like that for?' Archie asked as I came up the path.

'Because someone kindly put a handle at the top here.'

'Arr, but that's no reason for walkin' round 'oldin' it like a ruddy 'andbag. Get it up on thi shoulder, man, or tha'll rupture thissen. 'A'nt tha done any binnin' afore?'

'No!'

He sighed. Then, without warning, he snatched the bin from my grasp and threw it on to the ground. 'Watch!' he growled. From a half-kneeling position with one hand supporting the base he quickly stood up and the bin appeared miraculously upon his shoulder. It was all over before my fingers had realized the bin had gone.

'Reight, tha's seen it done now, nip. Only keep thi back straight or we'll be carryin' thee off i' two pieces. Now go an' empty it.'

He tossed the bin across on to my shoulder, and I felt the rim bite three inches deep into the flesh. I tottered round to the back of the lorry with Archie just behind me, and levered the bin over the sloping shelf. A storm of red-brown dust belched back in our faces, its breath sickly-sweet. We watched, perfectly still, as the great jaws chewed their way through several helpings of potato peelings and empty soap packets and finally swallowed a badly crumpled dustbin.

'Well,' Archie said, after a moment's reflection, 'This could turn aht to be an expensive day for ' ratepayers. Are tha bahn to do that wi' 'em all?'

'It was too heavy.'

'Tha should 'ave said.'

'It would still have been heavy. Anyhow, what do we do now?'

Archie thought for a minute.

'Fetch ' bin lid back 'ere an' chuck it on an' all, an' then let's scarper. That way, they'll know it's young vandals who's been. Ah'm not sayin' tha were wrong, kid, but don't do it again, 'cos if ' Fox gets to 'ear on it, tha'll wish tha'd gone in after it.'

As we set off again, Fatty Wishart lumbered alongside me, breathing heavily with that familiar death rattle in his throat shattering the quietness of the early morning.

'Tha 'eard what ' ganger said: don't lift it if it's too 'eavy; just tilt it a bit an' roll it. An' if it's too full to roll get someone to gie thi a 'and ... 'Cos don't thee worry, there's some bins even two men can't lift.'

'What do you do then?'

'Tha leaves it. That teaches 'em not to fill 'em so full.'

The gate squeals as you open it. Down the path. Bend. Hoist the bin. Up the path. The metal rim grinds out a jagged groove in your collar bone. The gate has grown tired of waiting and closed itself. You open it with one hand while the dustbin struggles to leap away over the garden. A frothing torrent of garbage grates and tinkles down the chute and the gritty spray washes over you with a stink both stale and rotten. Return the bin, then down the path. Bend. Hoist. On and on in never-ending circles, the same routine mile after gruelling mile, until your shoulder is red-raw and the bruises swelling and your arms and thighs are screaming to drop off and die. And everyone is hurrying to be finished, if a finish there be, so you hurry your failing legs along too. Never a halt. Bend. Hoist. Bend. Hoist.

'Don't thee be fooled just 'cos 'bin's only 'afe full,' Bill advised me as we came off Clifton Crescent. 'They're cunnin' swine, some folk. Tha picks it up casual like, 'cos tha thinks it's light, an' tha lands up on ' floor what wi' its bein' so 'eavy. When tha looks i'side, there's 'afe a dozen bricks 'idded at ' bottom. Sithee, look at this one. All tha sees is a few cardboard boxes. An' underneath ... Look! There's enough glass there to fill a green'ouse. Damned 'eavy glass. Tha can bet there's some bugger be'ind them curtains waitin' to bust aht laughin' when Ah does mi back in pickin' it up.'

'Ah'm nowt for class,' said Archie. 'Ah've been a Socialist ever sin' Ah can remember. But tha knows, there's allus less in t' bins o' them wi' brass than ' folks who's supposed to be poor. We'll be doin' some posh 'ouses today. Now, thee notice: all their waste food'll be wrapped up neat i' bags, an' all their tubes o' toothpaste'll be squeezed flat. Tha can carry them bins i' one hand. Then tha looks at ' council estates. Some o' bins's full o' tins 'cos she'd rather pay extra than bother 'ersen wi' cookin'. An' tha could make pies wi' ' jam they leave i' jars an' won't scrape aht. An' their bin stinks 'cos they nivver wrap owt up, so all ' gunge sticks to ' bottom. Oh arr, Ah've allus said it's them as can't afford to what wastes ' most.'

'They do it aht o' spite, some on 'em. There's a bloke on this 'ere street who's allus moanin' abaht 'ow 'igh 'is rent is. On a council estate an' all! So 'e gets 'is own back bi fillin' 'is bin reight up to ' rim every week: an' if 'e can't find enough, 'e tops it up wi' watter. 'E says it's just to make sure 'e gets value for 'is brass.'

A small, stout woman waddled down the path as we passed by, her crinkled lips sucked in between her toothless gums and her feet buried in bundles of blue, false fur.

'Take us mi mattress, love, will yer?'

'We're not furniture removers, Missis.'

'It's just in ' back doorway, look. It's not 'eavy.'

'Can't, love. Sorry. We just do dustbins, like. We 'a'nt room for nowt big.'

'Put it on ' top o' yer lorry. Yer lads can 'ave a pound for it.'

'Well ... It's risky ... Might not 'old ...'

The old woman merely digested her lips.

'All reight, love. Seein' as it's for a good cause.'

'Reight! Ah'll go an' get our dad to gie yer a 'and.'

'Silly, old bitch,' Archie said as she disappeared into the house. 'If she'd 'phoned ' depot, they'd've sent round ' spare wagon an' it'd 'ave cost 'er nowt. Tha knows, nip, some folk thinks tha's got to pay just to live.'

'And you've hardly enlightened her.'

'No. But for another quid Ah would.'

The shops were always difficult. They crammed the bins with large, cardboard boxes which then became wedged and you had to scoop everything out with your hands. Lifting them was often a two-man job. The butcher's backyard was almost solid with dustbins and for several minutes we were weaving in convoys through the queue of customers inside his shop until the stench drove most of them out on to the pavement. I looked back inside and saw the clouds of ash and Heaven knows what else slowly settling like the sheerest veil.

Laughing Gus poked me in the arm.

'An' then tha wonders why folk turn vegetarian.'

Bend. Hoist. Bend. Hoist.

Two hundred bins emptied and we are still not half way through the round. The bins become heavier and more unwieldy, and your limbs numb and uncooperative. The sweat runs freely and your face is crusted with the vomited dust from the lorry's gaping mouth. Your lips are parched and your tongue on an errand of mercy returns capped with grit and a burning taste of salt. And now the risen sun has turned the street into a furnace with not a breath of air, and you are continually shaking off a cloud of flies that come to lick the filth on your head and arms. And still you must wrestle with ancient bins with rusty, jagged edges and inconvenient holes that pour trickles of scum down your neck, with excited dogs guaranteed not to hurt a soul which nevertheless consider a dustman when he is helpless with a full bin on his back a finer delicacy than the ordinary postman, with washing lines like trip wires strung out invisibly across the sky wrenching the bins from your grasp and nearly dislocating your shoulder. Meanwhile, people are demanding to know why you forgot them last Tuesday or if it was you who sprained the lock on the gate or if, out of the two thousand bins which were emptied last week, you happened to notice Aunt Edie's coronation cup and saucer which was thrown away by mistake. You feel there is something they should know about themselves, but somehow you manage to keep it all secret and instead you pass on ... and on ... and on.

I came across the four of them again gathered in front of the gate to a jungle of a garden. It seemed appropriate to ask why.

'Just look at yon,' said Fatty, pointing to the house.

I looked. The dustbin was clearly visible by the back door, and there was nothing particularly wonderful about it. But behind the glass panels of the door was a St Bernard that had passed well beyond the stage of being full-grown, and he viewed our presence with loud displeasure.

'That's a nice dog,' I said, by way of surmise.

'Dog?! Don't talk daft, man! That's a bloody elephant wi' long

teeth. An' if tha thinks 'e's makin' some noise now, thee listen to
'im when tha tries goin' down ' path. Bi ' time tha's got to ' bin,
'e'll 'ave ' side o' ' 'ouse down. Well Ah'm not bahn down, Ah can
tell thee straight.'

'Where's his owner?'

'' way 'e's lookin' at us, Ah reckon 'e's eaten 'im an' likes '
taste,' said Laughin Gus.

'We're leavin' it,' decided Archie, striding off. 'An' we're not
comin' back till yon's be'ind bars. Come on! ... Ah say! Nip! Don't
thee go down Number Fourteen.'

'All right ... Why not?'

'Cos that's Fatty's.'

We saw Fatty duly disappearing behind Number Fourteen.

''E saw this bird an' 'er bloke goin' at it 'ammer an' tongs on t'
sofa two year sin', an' 'e reckons if 'e goes often enough 'e'll catch
'em at it again.'

'Why don't you go?'

'Ah've more sense. Besides, Ah know she moved a year back.'

'Why not tell Fatty, then?'

'Damned 'eavy bin, that.'

By snap-time we had laboured without a break for more than an
hour and even the most gruesome discharges could not now deflect
a growing appetite. We tumbled into the spacious cabin and
passively allowed its familiar, spicy fragrances of stale sweat,
garbage and engine oil set to work on our saliva glands. Five
bundles of sandwiches and five flasks appeared from the musty
depths of donkey jackets, overcoats and the dashboard; five pairs
of work-soiled hands grappled with crackling, white, paper bags;
five pairs of jaws tore greedily into slabs of bread and cheese, bread
and jam and plain sponge cake.

'Where's thine?' Bill asked me in between bites.

'I don't bring any.'

'Tha wants to get summat down thee. No wonder tha're built like
a piece o' string. Don't tha ever 'ave any snap?'

'No.'

'Tha mun be 'im as eats raw eggs, then,' said Fatty.

'Yes; I suppose so.'

'Bloody disgustin'!' Cyril observed, gustily.

'Nay, lay off ' kid,' said Archie. ''E does reight if that's 'ow 'e likes 'em. At least 'e's not as bad as Gus 'ere, wrappin' 'is snap up i' newspaper. For me, that's ' 'eight o' depravity. 'E's probably ' only bloke i' this country who reads 'is sandwiches afore 'e eats 'em.'

'Tha're wrong there,' Laughing Gus corrected him. 'Ah read 'em after. That's 'ow Ah learn. Ah just eat ' news an' then inwardly digest it.'

'Tha'll not 'ave to mind us, kid,' Archie said. 'It's allus like this. We've worked wi' Gus that long, we're as daft as 'im.'

''E wants to think 'issen lucky 'e came wi' us an' not Kendray lot. At t' speed they work, they'd 'ave 'im crippled in a week. We might turn folk balmy 'ere, but at least we send them 'ome i' working order.'

'Does tha know they might be losin' their driver? They've been told to go an' see Fox abaht it.'

'Why?' I asked.

''Cos every time 'e goes aht 'e gets 'em into trouble some'ow. Does tha know, 'e 'a'nt been wi' 'em above two week an' 'e nearly got 'em all t' sack ... It's reight what Ah'm tellin' thee! 'E pulls up by one o' ' shops on ' estate there, an' it's that one where they've five bins. Wuh, they'd only emptied four when this bread van comes up be'ind 'im delivering, like: so 'e just moves up ' road an' lets it come into 'is place. Then Bertie comes aht wi' ' last bin, an' baht lookin', daft sod chucks it into ' back o' ' bread van. 'E ruined every single loaf there were. It cost ' Corporation nearly forty quid to pay for 'em an' t' shopkeeper said if they didn't pay 'e'd put Bertie on ' bacon-slicer.'

'That's 'ow 'e works, tha sees. Allus edgin' up t' street to save time, like. 'E's even movin' while they're throwin' rubbish in. That's why they're in trouble now. One on 'em gets to ' back wi' a full bin an' 'e moves off just as an open sports car goes past, an' 'o course, ' passenger gets ' lot.'

'It's only 'cos they want to finish first every day, 'cos they think they're ' best crew. Now, where's ' sense i' that? We could all flog ussens to death if we wanted but we wouldn't get paid any more. It don't mean owt just 'cos tha finishes quickest. Any'ow, we used to be ' best crew when Gordon were 'ere. Even ' Kendray crew couldn't 'ave licked us then.'

'Aye! them were ' days. 'E were one o' these muscle men, tha knows. Third i' Mr United Kingdom. An' Mr Barnsley 'e were, three year runnin' ... An' tha meant it every time tha said it. Six-foot-six an' just as broad. Muscles like bricks. It used to be 'is trainin', this round. Tha'd see 'im run aht wi' a bin on each shoulder ... full bins, an' runnin'! 'E'd just chuck 'em in, throw, ' bins down on t' pavement an' run for ' next. All we 'ad to do were to take ' empties back, three of us, an' we'd all 'Ell on to keep up wi' 'im.'

'Aye! They all used to come aht o' their 'ouses to watch 'im. Otherwise 'e could 'ave done ' round on 'is own.'

'We'll 'ave thee trained to take 'is place, kid, by ' end o' ' week,' Bill jeered. 'Tha could do wi' puttin' some meat on. 'Ow's tha like thi first day 'ere, then? Ah bet thi shoulder 'urts like 'Ell, now, don't it?'

He squeezed it just inside the protruding end of my collar bone with expert precision. Searing fires flared beneath his heavy fingers, and my shirt, wedded to the skin with caked blood, ripped off the scabs and I could feel the wet patch spreading.

'What happened to him?'

'Who?'

'Gordon.'

Bill released his grip.

'Strongest man I ever knew.'

'Yes, but what happened to him?'

There was a prolonged silence, like Armistice Sunday.

''E went to be a dancer.'

'You mean like they have on musicals?'

'No! ...'

'What kind, then?'

'Well it were, um ...'

'What?'

'... Wuh ... like ballet.'

'Oh!'

'Arr! ... That were it ... That's what 'e left for any'ow.'

'... It were 'is ambition, like: what 'e wanted to do.'

'Yes.'

'Wouldn't do if we all wanted to be t' same, would it?'

We all fell into silence again.

''Course, we didn't 'ave a lot to do wi' 'im ahtside work.'

'No.'

'Nay, we knew nowt abaht it till 'e'd left ... 'an 'e weren't wi' us all that long, considerin'.'

'No.'

Another silence.

'But you couldn't do ballet if you were that shape.'

'Ah wouldn't know. But would tha 'ave risked tellin' 'im?'

The delicate 'tap-tap-tap' of a woman's heels passing by drew our attention outside. A fine pair of legs, held together by the briefest mini-skirt, tripped light as a feather away down the street, beneath a moving sea of rich, red hair shimmering under the morning sun.

'She could 'ave me any time she asked,' Fatty revealed dreamily.

'Nay, she's more than likely already got a garden gnome,' said Bill. 'Any'ow, Fatty, she'd turn thee into a seven stone weaklin' i'side an hour an' no question. Tha can tell she's no virgin.'

'How?'

'Bi just usin' thi eyes. Girls what's randy today don't mind what they show. They all go aht baht nylons, an' wi' ' bottom o' their skirts wrapped round their belly buttons. Just like 'er, there. Ah tell thee, young uns's that ripe nowadays tha don't even 'ave to peel 'em.'

'We were allus told tha could tell a virgin 'cos 'er eyes sparkled wi' innocence,' said Laughing Gus, slowly. 'Mind, it were Father O'Leary who told us an' Ah often wondered 'ow 'e fun aht.'

'Nay, tha's got it wrong way round, Gus. Tha should see their eyes sparkle when they've 'ad it.'

We laughed.

'Trouble wi' Gus is 'e's lived wi' 'is mother all 'is life. Tha'll not believe it, but does tha know, kid, 'e's thirty year old an' 'e's nivver 'ad it, 'as tha, Gus?'

'No.'

We all laughed again, helplessly and heartily. We could not stop laughing. Even Gus was laughing in a slightly sheepish fashion. We laughed until the tears poured down our cheeks and our sides ached, and the metal cabin rang and echoed with loud derision. It was, after all, so absurd, beyond belief; it was so funny it was almost unbearable, and we howled with frank abandon for we were all either married or under twenty-five.

'Aye! Thirty an' nivver 'ad it. ' nearest 'e's ever been to 'avin' a neet on ' tiles were when 'e were mendin' roof once an' 'is uncle broke ' ladder.'

'Tha wants to 'ave a neet out wi' that red'ead, yon, Gus. She'll put some 'air on thi chest.'

The cabin rocked to our uncontrollable hilarity. In the front seat Archie had laughed so much he had nearly swallowed his false teeth and was now choking violently. Behind him Fatty was almost paralytic with a hail of raucous bellows roaring out from one end, and a steady rhythm of ominously dull thuds from the other. Cyril's flask had just dislodged itself and filled his tobacco pouch to the brim.

'Tha'd nivver want for nowt again,' said Bill. 'She'd get thee while tha ... Jesus Christ! Fatty, are tha goin' bad? Where's tha dredged that up from?'

The offender dissolved into chuckles again, and from the depths a rapid boom like distant howitzers sent tremors shuddering across the back seat.

'Bloody 'Ell fire, Ah'm gettin' aht o' 'ere,' Archie croaked, half-suffocating. "E's either bahn to poison us or explode. An' for God's sake, don't anyone strike a match till Ah've got clear.'

Almost as one we tumbled outside, coughing and spluttering, sucking in the fresh, Barnsley air. Only Fatty remained inside shrieking his head off, with his rear end performing a rapid and deafening tattoo.

'By 'Ell, 'e could win prizes wi' them if ' judge could survive long enough,' said Cyril. "E mun 'ave been savin' them up for weeks.'

'Serves 'im reight if 'e's blown a 'ole in 'is breeches. If Ah can find a cork wide enough ...'

'Eee, mi sandwiches!' Laughing Gus wailed. 'Ah've left 'em in ' cab.'

'Tha can't eat 'em now,' said Cyril, looking in through the front window, 'they're curlin' up round ' edges.'

'It's time we were off an' all, now,' Archie said, consulting his watch.

'Well, unless tha can push ' lorry, we're stayin' 'ere,' Cyril told him. 'Ah'm not drivin' i' that, not now Ah've seen Gus's cheese go green.'

The minutes dragged by, and still the cannonade showed no

signs of abating. Archie kept looking at his watch and grew more and more desperate. At one point, muzzled by his handkerchief, he bravely threw open both doors to clear the air, but the result was so uncomfortable to those of us outside that Bill, in the interests of public health, slammed them shut. There was nothing for it but to stand outside and wait.

'We could 'ave done wi' 'im on ' Normandy beaches,' Cyril growled. 'We'd 'ave just pulled 'is breeches down, pointed 'is arse at ' Jerry lines, an' they'd 'ave surrendered on t' spot.'

Ten precious minutes passed before Cyril, having lit his pipe and built up a good head of smoke inside the cabin by blowing through a small window, ventured cautiously back into his seat, and one by one we followed. Well behind schedule we shot off down the street, Cyril still puffing furiously and visibility consequently reduced to zero, while Fatty, banished for his sins to the platform at the rear of the vehicle, chuckled merrily at everyone on the footpath who turned round to wonder what on earth was fouling that lorry's exhaust.

7 Further Education

Had it not been for the seasonal migration of about a dozen students to swell the numbers of the Barnsley dustmen the town might well have been submerged beneath the wastes of summer. Absenteeism in the department always stood at a very healthy level, but from July to September it reached raging proportions, rarely falling below thirty per cent of the work force. Of course, holidays accounted for much of the drop in labour, but it was curious to note that weather warm enough to bring the fish to the surface at the same time invariably blighted the men with a dreadful plague, while during Doncaster Race Week well-beloved aunts died in their scores. Every Monday the Fox posted statistics of the previous week's non-attendances outside the inspector's office, although as a gesture that was not demonstrably sympathetic, it was effectively countered by everyone completely ignoring it. At the bottom of the notice was a reminder that anybody who was absent for a total of more than thirteen weeks in the year had to report for a medical examination. Stan often said, almost with pride, that this measure had never been necessary, but the fact remained that, to their credit, many kept in good health by only a matter of days.

Normally, students just used to fill in temporary gaps within the regular crews, but on that particular day, and to everybody's surprise, there was almost a full turn-out, so that faced with such unexpected enthusiasm the Cleansing Department ran out of jobs before men. By the time the yard had emptied itself of barrows and carts there were still three students, Brian, Chris and me, holding up the porch, with Brian occasionally ringing the bell on the clocking-on machine and shouting 'Shop!' It was by no means easy for Mike to find work for us. All the tools disposed about the place were in various states of disrepair, and for Chris, who was six feet tall only when he sat down, giving him the brush that Willie had chewed the top off was like expecting anybody else to sweep the street with a toothbrush. Eventually, however, we came upon two weather-beaten hand-carts slowly disintegrating on the rubbish heap, and fitted them out with brushes suffering from bristle-rot and shovels with blades like rip-saws. Chris and I had by far the better bargain; at least its only flaw was a twisted axle so that it tried to run down both sides of the road at once. Brian's, on the other hand, looked old enough to be Boadicea's chariot and threw off side-panelling or a bin at regular intervals. We were now nearly half-an-hour behind the rest and conscience spurred us to make a hasty departure before the Fox became aware of our delay. Brian rattled out of the yard some ten yards ahead of us at a brisk canter. Suddenly, the noise of his passage was drowned by screaming brakes, and we dashed round the corner to see his barrow gliding gracefully across to the other side of the road while Brian was perching in a somewhat makeshift fashion on the bonnet of a Ford Cortina. The driver, an extremely attractive middle-aged woman, was leaning, white as death, out of the window addressing him in cultured tones with a flow of phrases you would not otherwise have expected her to understand.

'I wonder what she was trying to tell me,' said Brian, as the car sped away.

'I couldn't follow it all,' Chris confessed, 'But she seemed inclined to the view that your steering could be improved by major surgery.'

'Perhaps I did get it wrong, then,' Brian said, sadly. 'I thought it was just her way of saying, "Come up and see me, sometime".'

It was just starting to drizzle when we left Brian at the entrance to Beevor Hall, but by the time we began to climb the hill to Cundy Cross, there was a steady downpour. Charlie and Fred stood watching us from the top, sheltering under the wall of a public lavatory.

'How is it you've only got here when you had half-an-hour's start on us?'

'We've further than thee to go, nip. It takes us longer, tha sees.'

Now the rain was coming down heavily, so at Charlie's suggestion we sought a more convenient shelter. There was an empty council house a little way along, and after Charlie had forced the kitchen window with instructive, if not discomfortingly obvious, skill, we all climbed inside, boots first, in a clumsy scramble which did nothing to enhance the appearance of the enamel sink unit. We had only been there long enough for Fred to find a two-shilling piece lodged under the dining-room fireplace when a pinched, woman's face, wrapped up in a brown, threadbare shawl, thrust itself through the window.

'What are you doin' 'in 'ere?'

Charlie and Fred looked at each other with expressive amazement.

'Are tha talkin' to me or them?' Charlie asked.

'Ah'm talkin' to all of you.'

'Ee, Ah think that's clever. It's more than Ah could do. Mind, Ah've only got one mouth.'

'Ah want none o' your sauce. You've no right to be 'ere. This is private property.'

'What are tha doin' 'ere, then?'

'Ah've come to see what you're up to.'

'Well, if tha must know, we've come to turn aht this 'ere gas fire.'

'But it's not lit.'

'No, but it will be if Ah can find ' mains tap.'

'Look! Either you come out or Ah fetch ' bobbies.'

'You mean we can stay in if they come,' said Chris.

'All right, cheeky sods, Ah'll report you all, then. This belongs to ' Council ...'

'Tha're reight. We're from ' Council, an' this is a Council meeting.'

'You've no business 'ere.'

'An' we've just resolved that due to extreme weather conditions makin' us tea go cold Ah'm bahn to shut this bloody window.'

He closed it with such force it almost unzipped her nose; then he proceeded to clear his throat over the sink.

'You've done it now,' I said, as she stormed off pouring out a stream of promises on behalf of her husband and half-a-dozen policemen. 'She's certain to report you.'

'Let 'er,' Charlie said, with calm philosophy. 'They'll not find aht it's me. Our patch is up at Lundwood. Ah was nivver 'ere as far as them's concerned.'

'Very shrewd,' I said, settling down on the floor like the rest. 'But someone's going to get a surprise. Whose patch is it?'

He took a huge bite out of his sandwich.

'Thine.'

Somehow we ended up by swapping wartime experiences,

although as Chris and I were born in the late forties our contributions were comparatively small. Charlie Gosport had had a distinguished military career, being decorated twice for bravery through the good fortune of having a namesake in his battalion prepared to take on the whole enemy front line single-handed while he, Charlie, organised a one-man retreat behind the First Aid Unit whenever the guns opened fire. He received an early discharge, and later a War Pension, as a result of being severely wounded early in 1945 — by a poisoned bayonet, for official purposes — but in fact by a German frau who skewered him in the backside with a rusty pitchfork while he was raping her daughter.

On the other hand, Fred was an ardent pacifist on the grounds of self-preservation and, although he found the bombing and rationing somewhat disruptive, firmly believed that, if he pretended they were not there, the war and the nasty Germans would all go away. With commendable ingenuity he avoided conscription by taking a series of vital jobs — and from which he was dismissed without exception for incompetence — while his main contribution to the war effort appeared to take the form of boosting the morale of half-a-dozen women whose husbands were away fighting for their common survival. By a curious irony he received his call-up papers on VJ-Day, but it was only after an unsuccessful attempt to gas himself that the implications hit home.

It was nearly eleven o'clock before the final details of how Britain won the war were fitted into place, and with the coming of victory came also, with dramatic effect, the sun. Charlie and Fred took themselves off to Lundwood, leaving Chris and me to secure the premises as best we could. Out in the open again we found the gutters and alleyways had been transformed into streams of oozing mud. At the best of times, a day spent scanning interminable lengths of dreary, grey pavement has little to provide in the way of excitement, but when all you can see are the dark, thickening drifts of slime while the wind blows cold over you and the drizzle makes your clothes damp, the effect is soul-destroying. Every swing of the brush drags to a halt in the mud: every shovelful of earth hangs as deadweight. The fine dust that whisked away in the breeze now spatters your boots and cakes your trouser-bottoms. We toiled for half an hour or so, and the impression we made grew less and less as the conditions became more difficult and depressing until, finally, the bottom of

Chris's shovel fell out. He swore politely.

'A good workman never blames his tools,' I reminded him.

'That's his damned fault,' he replied. 'It's no wonder he never gets promotion if he can't blame his mistakes on someone else.'

Five minutes later the head of the brush I was using split in two.

'Now you can work twice as hard,' said Chris, and leaning on his brush to laugh at his own joke, snapped the shaft.

'Blood and sand!' he rasped. 'Whoever used this barrow last must have been a leper. Let's get it back to the depot before we turn into a pile of limbs.'

The episode was regarded with something approaching derision by those who were already in the canteen when we arrived there at mid-day. Jake, who had brought us back in the spare wagon, had lost no time in telling the tale while we slipped away for our fish and chips, so that our return was greeted by shaking heads and a round of wry smiles. Even the most idle amongst them knew better than to pull a ruse that was so obvious. There were bound to be repercussions.

But we were in no mood for friendly warnings. On the way back from the fish shop we had nipped through the hole in the fence as usual to avoid the long haul round by the main entrance. For some time past a stray mongrel, whose spirit of enterprise was marred only by his lack of good manners, had formed the habit of standing by the opening from twelve o'clock onwards and aggressively demanding a toll of a fair-sized chip from anyone passing through. Usually it was sufficient just to cast one over his head and then run like the wind for the canteen, but on this occasion he had simultaneously experienced a loathing for chips and a partiality for leg meat, and as mine happened to be the only piece handy, he bit it. Chris, who was behind me, being afraid that it might tear his trousers too, darted back through the gap while a rusty nail made a six inch rip across his seat. So we paid scant attention to their witticisms until Stan came in with a message from the Fox that we were to transfer our robust energies that afternoon to a certain street in Lundwood whose reputation in Barnsley matched that of the Gorbals in Glasgow.

'What did Ah tell thee?' crowed Basil, as the sneers and guffaws died down. 'That's for breakin' 'is brushes. Tha'll be beggin' 'im to let thee pay for 'em bi four o'clock.'

'But Charlie and Fred sweep Lundwood,' I protested.

'We 'a'nt done that street i' months,' said Charlie.

'Why not?'

''Cos it's mucky.'

'But it will be if you don't clean it.'

'It's mucky when tha does clean it, i'nt it, Fred? They wait till tha's gone past, an' then they bring all their rubbish aht an' chuck it on t' street. They seem to like it that way.'

'An' another thing,' Harry Jagger warned us. 'Don't put thi brush down or it's ' last tha'll see on it. ' last time 'e sent students up there, they came back wi' nowt. Young uns 'ad nicked everythin' for scrap, barrow an' all, baht anyone seein' 'em.'

The cards span from his hands around the table as he spoke, flicking over the little piles of pennies. They were playing a form of twelve-card brag where the well-worn quality of the cards had overlaid the skill of the brag with an open opportunity to calculate the value of every other player's hand. We students were playing bridge on the opposite table, not because we found it intellectually more satisfying but because it had become obvious over a period of time that our involvement in twelve-card brag was being met with more than chance.

'Tha nivver knows,' said Fatty Booth. 'Tha might be as lucky as me when Ah were up there last. Ah were comin' down ' street, an' there were this 'ere woman stood at 'er front window. An' Ah'm just lookin', when she sees me an' takes 'er blouse off, an' she's no bloody bra' on!'

'What did you do?'

''E were sick on t' spot, that's what 'e did: Ah saw 'im just after,' Joss intervened.

'Arr, well, she looked well ovver sixty,' Fatty explained, reddening slightly, 'An' big an' fat — an' great tits like sacks o' soggy porridge. That's what put me off.'

'Tha're wastin' thi breath warnin' 'em, Fatty. No bird'll look twice at a couple o' long 'aired yobboes like them. Tha wants to get rid on it, yawh two.'

'It came as part of the set.'

'Listen 'ere. Does tha know scientists 'ave proved it's thi 'air that stops thi bein' sexy? Ah mean, just look at these bald 'eaded blokes — virile as bloody bulls, aren't they? Women go mad for 'em, 'cos they know what they can do. Now if tha 'as 'air, it stands to reason whilever it grows it's sappin' thi strength ... It's no different from prunin' thi plants: ' more suckers tha cuts off, ' better t' flower. That's why Ah keep it like this' — he paused to scratch the dense cap of bristling spikes — 'An' it's done me proud. When Ah first 'ad it done, our lass didn't know what 'ad 'it 'er.'

'Well why not cut your arms and legs off as well, then? On your reckoning, that should save you enough strength to take on a harem.'

'Nay, lay off. Does tha know, Arthur, young nip came round wi' me t'other week, an' we went round almost every shop an' supermarket i' Barnsley: there were lasses o' all shapes an' sizes, an' 'e didn't get off wi' one on 'em. Tha can't get 'em goin', nip, when thi 'air looks like an Afghan rug. They know tha'll 'ave worn thissen aht just gettin' thi 'ead off ' pillow. Show 'em them photos tha's got, Joss, so they know what Ah'm tryin' to tell 'em.'

The words had hardly shaken free from his lips before Joss found himself besieged by a crowd of men whose bulging eyes and quickening breath spoke well of their thirst for knowledge too. Several years ago, while on a naval visit to Hong Kong, he had acquired a batch of photographs at a bargain price capturing the occasion of two very attractive young women entertaining an enormous Chinaman in their private quarters, and now and then, he would bring down a sample on a kind of spontaneous exhibition, a very popular event. Today's was no exception. There were half-a-dozen snaps all told in which the group struck various poses that would have ruptured all but the world's top gymnasts. From sweaty palm to shaking fingers they passed. According to Joss the two girls were the wives of military personnel stationed in the Far East, and this rather open exercise was just a means of escape for them when they were bored with life, but, as Chris observed, a pretty female was extremely unlikely to avoid that feeling by jumping into bed with any man worth his salt.

'Does tha see what Ah mean, now?' Harry asked. 'Bald as a brass knob 'e is. An' 'as tha seen two lasses wi' 'appier, smilin' faces anywhere?'

'Tha wants to get 'old o' one o' ' birds Fatty gets off wi',' Arthur advised us. 'That'd show thee a bit o' life. Tha gets some real randy uns, don't tha, Fatty?'

'Arr!' said Fatty, puffing out with unassuming pride. 'Ah'm off

aht wi' one toneet, who Ah met up Town End just now. A real sexy
piece, an' all, blonde, wi' long eyelashes, black, leather boots wi'
'igh 'eels an' a chest like a prize pigeon.'

'Tha're all reight there, Fatty. Can't tha find one like that for
these two lads?'

'Arr. Well ... Ah tell thee what, nip. Tha can 'ave this one Ah'm
tellin' thee abaht. Ah forgot Ah were bahn aht wi' another bird
toneet an' all.'

'That's very kind of you, but ...'

'She's bahn to wait for me bi ' garage on Summer Lane at seven.
Just say Ah can't come an' Ah've sent thee.'

'Does she like it, Fatty?' shouted Basil.

'Oh arr! 'Ot an' strong. That's 'ow she likes it. Can tha manage
'er, kid?'

'I'm extremely touched, Fatty, but ...'

'Nay, Ah'd better go. Tha'd nivver do it as well as me. Any'ow,
she'd go off thee as soon as tha opened thi gob: tha talks like a
ponce.'

Charlie and the rest had not been exaggerating over lunch about
what we should find at Lundwood. The street was one long litter
basket, while the smaller, conventional refuse bins that had been
fitted to the lamp-posts had long since found their way to the back
door of a scrap-metal merchant. There were pools of sludge
spreading across the pavements, smothering a welter of cigarette
packets, cans and newspapers. What surprised us most, however,
was the enormous number of broken beer bottles that lay scattered
about. The dustmen who knew the place best explained that the men
here — and some of the women — used to leave the pub at closing
time carrying bags full of beer to round off the evening at home, but
were so drunk by then that most of it finished down the gutter, and as
for the rest they were the legacies of Saturday night brawls. Barney,
who lived not far away, said that no-one dared to buy a new car
there, since anything strange left out in the street after dusk would be
torn out of recognition by morning. It was in this secluded
atmosphere that we set to work. Almost from the beginning we were
surrounded by a horde of dirty, unkempt children who seemed
keener to keep the rubbish out of the barrow rather than in it, so that
there was more room there for themselves. It was not easy to stop
them with a brush in one hand and a shovel in the other, which we

dare not put down for fear that they would vanish. In the end we let the children decide how clean the streets would be. As for Fatty's friend, who subsequently acquired fame throughout Barnsley as 'Old Porridge Tits', she was too modest that afternoon even to come to the window, but her place was readily taken by a very shapely and scantily-clad nymph who followed us along the street and occasionally sat upon the wall in a fashion which left little to the imagination. It was only because Chris's brother had taught at the local school that we could appreciate that her blatant maturity made a mockery of her thirteen years.

Neither of us possessed a watch, but time sped by and we seemed to have only begun when we spotted Charlie and Fred moving along Pontefract Road at a very comfortable pace back to the depot. It rather took us by surprise that it was time to finish already, but we immediately gave chase with a stream of yelling, scruffy urchins racing round us trying to drag off the brushes or the bins, like half-starved wolves pursuing the legendary sleigh over the Russian snows. By the time we had literally shaken them off we had reached the brow of the hill at Cundy Cross and our quarry was a matter of a few yards away. Just then, the bar joining the handles, with which Chris had been steering, came away in his hands, and with a rusty chuckle the barrow slipped away towards its smarter mate. Charlie and Fred watched with polite interest as it slowly rumbled up to them, all but ran over their feet and then, picking up speed, raced for the valley.

'Thi barrow's loose,' Charlie warned us.

The barrow almost threw itself down the hill. Pausing only to express a few choice hopes about Charlie's future prospects, Chris ran after it and so swiftly that he caught up with it long before our fellow sweepers had found a perch from which to follow events. But by then the runaway had gathered sufficient momentum to make any immediate attempt to arrest it a free opportunity to lose both arms. So, Chris ran along with it, his lanky frame bent almost double, because the remains of the handles were below his knees. No doubt he can laugh at the memory of it now, but while he was hurtling down the central white line in this curious posture, with oncoming traffic brushing his elbow, his one burning ambition was to find a large unoccupied lavatory. By superb reflex action, however, he arrived at the bottom unscathed and came to rest on a pile of earth that Brian had just swept together.

'What the 'Ell's that?' Charlie asked, pointing to Brian's barrow as we reached them.

The barrow, whose health had been suspect early that morning, was rapidly fading. Two side-panels had disappeared; so had one of the bins, while the other had split down one of the edges.

'I've not decided, yet,' Brian replied. 'I'm thinking of calling it "Man With Dog", but I'm having problems with the wheels. What are you doing going back this early for?'

It turned out to be not yet three o'clock, but Charlie explained it was good practice to make sure you were not late in clocking-off so that the clerical staff could get away on time. We saw the force of this and spent the best part of half-an-hour, just out of consideration for them, behind the wall at the last bend before the depot. At a quarter-to-four we moved out on to the deserted road, and in a matter of seconds a convoy of six barrows poured out from Oakwell Lane, four more trundled under the bridge from the town centre and two others rolled out of Langdale Road. Their precision was almost superhuman. They could not have rehearsed it better. I probably looked as surprised as I felt.

'Well, nip,' said Charlie, with a wise smile kindling his wrinkled, weatherbeaten face, 'Thee tell me a job where folks don't.'

8 The Spare Wagon

Several changes had occurred at the depot during the few weeks I was away on holiday, so the place seemed strange when I returned. Tug Spooner had left to work in a carpet factory at Darton, not many miles away, because wages were higher and his uncle was one of the managers. New warehouses for fruit and vegetables — the Covent Garden of Barnsley — were rising from the very middle of the yard, and it was going to be a most comforting thought for some to know that their weekly groceries had recently rubbed shoulders with much of the festering refuse of the borough. On the other hand, most of the routine matters had altered little. Lampy was still fighting for better dinner-hours; Fatty Booth had a new, amorous, and transparently fictitious, adventure to relate every lunch-time in the canteen; and the Kendray crew were continually rushing themselves into trouble. On the very day I came back, they were summoned before the Superintendent. Apparently, one of the team had gone on ahead as usual and had lined up bins on the edge of the pavement from one end of a street to the other, but the rest had, in the hurry to finish, forgotten to go down there. The result was that later that day, high winds emptied the bins on their behalf, garnished the hedges and flowerbeds with potato peelings and newspaper, and tinted everything from the lawns to the bedroom windows with a fine, delicate-pink ash.

The man of the moment, however, was Harry Jagger. He had recently left the cardboard lorry to be the driver for the Kendray crew. (Their previous driver had been transferred after inching up the road with his eye on the activity at the rear of the lorry while his front nearside wheel slowly crushed a senior citizen's foot.) In the same week Harry started his new job the Corporation took delivery of two new, giant dustbin-lorries and put one of them into service on the Kendray round. Harry was so proud he was making all the crew wipe their feet before they got into it. But on the fourth day, he left the dumping area at Lundwood with the body still in a tipping position, and as he went under the railway bridge before Hoyle Mill, half a mile away, most of the lorry parted company with him, and six thousand pound's-worth of British workmanship was converted into instant scrap. It had surprised no-one that Harry was now back on the cardboard lorry.

At that time I had begun working on the spare wagon with Jake and Barney. No-one knew how it came by that name — although the driver before Jake had been in the habit of taking his girl friends for a ride in it — but its work involved a sort of general, dogsbody removal service, dismantling heaps of rubble which appeared, often mysteriously, in alleyways, collecting household furniture that even the most desperate second-hand dealer refused to touch, and so forth. They were good days, just riding around town when we did not feel like working, with Jake and Barney in the cabin and me standing on the back of the lorry and the cold wind on my face, or bouncing down the road on a bed three feet deep in cloth clippings from the tailor's. The very nature of the job made supervision impossible, and we, aware of the heavy burden of trust placed upon us, abused it to the full.

The three of us had worked solidly for an hour throwing bricks on to the lorry from a pile outside some garages in Princess Street. As Barney was sweeping up the last fragments, the garage owner who had made the complaint came across with a very embarrassed grin.

'Yer've done a good job,' he complimented us. 'Ah wonder if yer'd mind takin' a few flagstones we've got in our back garden. We've 'ad ' path taken up, yer see ...'

'Well, our worksheet just says "Rubble at garage in ..." '

'Aye, well. Ah were just askin'. Ah know that's yer job. Ah don't want to get yer doin' summat yer shouldn't ... Oh! ' wife wants to know if yer all take milk an' sugar in yer coffee.'

'We all 'ave both; two spoons for me,' replied Jake.

'Reight. It'll not be five minutes.'

There were rather more than a few flagstones round the back — in fact it looked as though he had walked off with a hundred yards of pavement from somewhere — and as we fought against their weight it occurred to me that this gaunt shadow of a man might have experienced some difficulty without someone to take up the garden path. But the ample form of his young daughter lay stretched out halfway between the stones and the lorry in a bikini that seemed hardly worth the trouble, and the operation very quickly developed into a keenly fought contest as to who could fetch the most.

It was she who brought the coffee as we rested on the lawn, bending before us with an obvious leisureliness which it seemed offensive to ignore.

'Did tha see ' knockers she'd got on 'er?' said Barney. 'If she'd come any closer she'd 'ave been stirrin' mi coffee wi' 'em. She mun use a bike pump to get 'em that size.'

'Ah know. Ah got a reight sweat on,' Jake added. 'Ah were fair worried one on 'em would fall aht an' belt me. Ah'm just wonderin' now if bein' 'it by a tit counts as an industrial injury.'

'Tha wants to stick wi' us, kid,' Barney advised me. 'Ah've a feelin' it's bahn to be like this all mornin'.'

But his hopes were short-lived. At the next call we made, in Derwent Drive, where we were supposed to remove a dining-room suite, the lock had been smashed, the place was deserted and there was not a stick of furniture to be seen; and at the address after that on our list, they had even taken the house.

They were an odd couple, Jake and Barney, Jake with his thinning red hair and a merry twinkle in his eye, his easy manners and flowing humour, Barney, by contrast, clumsy in his movements, slow-witted and permanently sour. Being such good friends they were always arguing: they would shout against one another until the cab rang with deafening echoes, Jake because he could run rings round Barney in any argument, Barney because he could shout louder. Usually, the cause was Barney's bad memory. He was always forgetting things, the names of people with whom he worked, the worklist, his new address — and he forgot to come to work at least once a fortnight — but what fouled Jake's temper most was Barney insisting upon calling at places where we had already been an hour or so before. It was not Barney's fault entirely. While he was completing a routine call at the age of seven, the lavatory cistern fell on his head, and apart from an unsociable reluctance to pull the flush ever again the result was that his memory emptied itself just as often as his bladder. The incident also did much to explain his small, squat features.

If they quarrelled about anything else it was nearly always because of Barney's wholesale claims upon anything going on the wagon which was not reduced to rubble or ash. Of course, everyone in the Department occasionally took home the odd item which took his fancy while he was sifting through the rubbish. Jake himself had sometimes put to one side a vase or a lampshade as we removed unwanted furniture. But Barney wanted everything; what was everybody else's waste was manna from heaven to him, and hardly a day passed when we did not throw a carpet roll or some planks of wood into the field where he kept his goats. He nearly had us all killed once when we came out of a factory with the cabin knee-deep in large plastic pipes which had excited his imagination — we were almost at the bottom of Market Hill when the lorry suddenly accelerated, scattered shoppers and a traffic warden on a zebra crossing and almost cut a bus in half because Jake, kicking frantically at a mound of tubes, could not find the brake. Nobody knew what Barney did with his treasures: Jake thought he fed the goats on them.

The only time I ever saw them come to blows, however, was when we were emptying dustbins at Carlton. This job had become a regular event after the second of the new dustbin-lorries had been allocated to the Carlton crew, for it was too wide to get down some of the lanes and so as an alternative to carrying the odd bin or two a quarter of a mile from a farm or a group of houses up to the main road, the binners forgot about them. Once a week we made the trip around the places that had been left, but it was not easy hauling a full dustbin over the back of a lorry seven feet above the ground. On this occasion, Barney had just handed a bin up to Jake, who was standing on the wagon, when the bottom dropped out and Barney emerged from the red-brown cloud dripping in cabbage stalks and covered from head to foot in cinders. Somehow he thought it was Jake's fault that the bin was defective, and with his eyes white with fury in his new, dusky complexion, he made several unsuccessful assaults on the wagon promising to make a few adjustments to Jake's face. Then, remembering the eggs we were delivering for Harry, who was off work with laryngitis, he fetched them out of the cab and pelted Jake with so many he looked like a walking omelette. In the end, Jake launched himself on to his opponent, just like they do in the films, and a battle-royal ensued in the best British traditions of no holds barred, feet first and hit where it hurts most. Luckily, before any serious damage had been done, the fight ended as they were attempting to castrate each other by a rather primitive manual method, for they both tumbled into a bunch of nettles and a frantic search then began for enormous quantities of dock leaves. For days afterwards, Barney would not even speak to either of us, but eventually his mind grew tired of the incident and blacked it out.

There were many times when we were called upon to do work which was really unpleasant. One day, we had come across the squashed remains of a black labrador lying in the road, and Barney and I had felt quite sick as we swung its stiff, heavy body over the lorry side with its eyeballs and innards dangling from it and wrapping themselves round our limbs. Just then, with a sense of timing that was positively uncanny, Mike O'Grady drove up to tell us to collect a number of dead dogs that had fallen off a lorry going to the glue factory. Barney had to be physically prevented from hitting him with a shovel. We spent the rest of the morning hunting all over Barnsley for these ghastly corpses, which were rotting and stinking and teeming with insect life, while Barney, whose ankle frequently gave way in times of stress, twisted it once again and left the undertaking to Jake and me. On the other hand, the job had its compensations. Often, when the strain of our labours proved too much, we would find a secluded spot away from the roadside and lie on the grassy banks on pillows of buttercups, with ferns and foxgloves gently waving above us, listening to the song of the lark as it soared into the deep-blue sky. Once we overslept, and arrived back at the depot long after everyone had gone home, but instead of getting our cards at the end of the week, as we all expected, we received an hour's overtime and not a word of inquiry.

At one time, while Jeth was foreman, we used to spend many of these afternoons resting at the salvage depot in Pogmoor, for Jeth used to supply us with mugs of fresh tea from his home in return for our placing his bets with a bookmaker in town. But he had been caught removing the engine of a car which had been dumped on the edge of the tip there and had been reduced to the ranks as a roadsweeper, while Pat, who had been helping him at the time but had got away, had been promoted to his place. With Pat there was always that nagging feeling of uneasiness. One Monday the Fine Fare supermarket reported that its refrigerators had broken down over the week-end and all the stock in them had to be destroyed. We took everything up to the incinerator in the salvage depot, and Pat went home with enough chicken, beef slices, peas and butter to see him and his family through until Christmas. Yet the next day, he told us that a friend had seen the spare wagon coming out of a scrap-metal merchant's yard, and suggested that in the interests of safety the proceeds of any transaction we conducted at such places on behalf of the Corporation should be split four ways and not three. So we avoided Pogmoor as much as possible and eventually discovered another sanctuary with a ready supply of tea at a sewage farm on the outskirts of Barnsley.

It was unfortunate that Pat had learned of our secret, but there was little to fear from someone making such a tidy sum from the sale of Corporation pornography to the owners of fish-and-chip shops. Besides, there was hardly anybody in the force who did not supplement his earnings with what might be termed a private income: what the others resented was that in our case there was so much greater opportunity. Some of it came to us as tips, and we always did a good job where we could expect gratitude in the form of hard cash, but we really preferred people to make their arrangements with us directly rather than through the Council because there was more profit in it. It was through these financial reasons that the rate for a job on the spare wagon became divided into two — fast and slow. We took matters more leisurely when we were working for the Corporation, going through the items listed on the daily worksheet. Our services as Corporation employees, however, were free only to those who lived in council houses — for reasons the social justice of which might escape many ratepayers who own their own homes — so it was often an advantage to deal with us on an informal basis because our charges were so much lower. Perhaps just as important a reason was that we worked faster when on our own account: we had to, so as to reduce the chances of being seen.

But these were all mere trifles. The major part of our takings came from a steady trade in the sale of scrap metal. What with people ridding themselves of Yorkshire ranges, iron bedsteads, ovens, fenders and the like in the rush to go modern, we were picking up half a lorry-load of metal a day to send down the tip, which seemed such a waste when the steel industry was so desperately short of raw material. Surprisingly, our thrifty intentions did not meet everywhere with approval, and despite the obvious boost to a failing economy, we were always hampered by the limited size of the market. There were some dealers who tottered on the verge of a stroke at the mere sight of a Corporation vehicle on the premises. Nevertheless, an enlightened few took what we had to offer with no questions asked and with ever-open doors. We always went late in the afternoon when we had accumulated sufficient stock, carefully placed near the tailboard for rapid unloading, and we would drive round and round the block until the coast was clear before charging into the yard while the wooden gates closed miraculously behind us. In fact, there were just sufficient traders interested in doing business for us to cast around for the best price. Even so, we were robbed hand over fist, for disposing of someone else's property did not put us in a very strong bargaining position, and in any case, once you have pulled several hundredweight of cast-iron off a lorry and then dragged them over to the scales for weighing it takes very strong reasons to persuade you to lift everything back again. In the circumstances, however, we could hardly complain, and in a situation where we held the upper hand we could be equally ruthless. One day, for instance, we called at a house in Monk Bretton to pick up some broken concrete slabs.

'Oi, lad!' the man called to me while the others were struggling down to the wagon, 'Can yer take this 'ere bedstead Ah've got i' ' garage?'

I was on the point of pulling it out through the doors when Jake, who had plainly overheard, hurried back to us.

'Sorry, mate. We can't take that. Concrete slabs. That's all we can take.'

The man's careless manner instantly solidified into caution. I could not believe my ears. It was an extremely heavy frame, and even I could see it was worth the best part of a pound to us.

'Why? It won't take up much room. An' it'll save yer 'avin' to make two journeys.'

'Arr, but it's ' Town 'All invoicin', tha sees. If Ah get caught wi' summat on ' wagon Ah'm not supposed to 'ave, Ah get ' sack, see.'

'Tell yer what, then. Ah'll gie yer thirty bob for yer trouble.'

'Ee no! Ah daren't risk ' sack ...'

The man thrust two pound notes into Jake's palm.

''Ere. Take this. Ah'll see thee reight if they ask any questions.'

'So tha sees, tha's got to use thi noddle a bit, nip,' said Jake as he divided the proceeds in the cab, 'Ah mean, look at it this way: 'e wants to get shut on it as much as ' scrap-dealers want thee to flog it 'em. It's t' same as Ah say: if tha's got two legs, why 'op?'

Nearly all the pieces we collected were made either of iron or steel, but we also went out of our way to bring in as much of the rarer metals as we could because the price was more favourable. While we were basking in the afternoon sun one day in the corner of a large, fallow field, we came upon a quantity of lead sheeting, which had fallen into a deep hole under the hedge, and it fetched ten pounds in one of the quickest deals of all time. Not many days later Jake uncovered a pile of battered aluminium saucepans in the bailing sheds by the Superintendent's office, and after a thorough search we added a teapot and some crumpled pewter plates. On the following day, just after the dinner hour, Barney told us to wait by the hole in the fence near the canteen. Ten minutes later, he appeared with a large copper containing a complete set of brass hearth utensils, some brass ornaments, a copper kettle, an electric kettle, a steel tray and a medium-sized paraffin stove, and wasted no time in throwing them on to the back of the wagon.

'Where's tha fun that lot?' Jake asked.

'At back o' bailin' shed.'

'But we looked all round there yesterday,' Jake objected.

'Arr, but Ah just thowt on a special place where we 'adn't looked, an' they were there.'

So, marvelling at Barney's shrewdness, we quickly disposed of them on highly reasonable terms. It was not until the week after that we heard that the clerical staff at the depot had lately been unable to make their morning coffee because someone had stolen their kettle. Not only that, they had lost several ornaments and an oil heater from the main office, and the thief had even gone into the Superintendent's room and walked off with a large copper coal-scuttle, leaving the contents scattered all over the carpet. Jake was furious at the news, and ranted and raved at Barney in language boiling with abusive hostility. But it was no use. By that time Barney had forgotten all about it, and Jake's behaviour only left him mystified.

Tuesday was always a good day, particularly when it was fine, for our first call in the afternoon was always to empty the dustbins at the recreation centre at Carlton. Not that this was an especially satisfying diversion: the bins were, as it happened, kept on the edge of a boggy patch, and you had only to pick one up for the place to come alive with tiny frogs pouring out of the top and cats leaping around your legs in their efforts to catch them. Sometimes Barney would go down the drive with a large bull-frog perched proudly in the centre of his flat cap. The real attraction, however, was to be able to lie on the gentle slopes and lightly doze away the hours or idly watch the children playing: from the middle of summer onwards we also had the pre-season advantage of seeing Barnsley's football team being put through its paces there.

'Just listen at ' grunts an' groans,' said Jake, as they trotted round the track for the umpteenth time. 'They're not fit to be out of their oxygen tents, none on 'em. Ah can't see us doin' much this year i' ' league, any'ow. They couldn't take on a team of old grannies, this lot.'

'Tha can see now why we're only i' Division Four.'

'Nay, it beats me 'ow we're even there when they're fallin' abaht like this. Some o' this lot won't see ' year aht at this rate. Ah've seen bigger thighs on sparrows. An' tha should see 'em play; runnin' up an' down ' field like zombies, an' then trip ovver ' ball as soon as kick it. Mind, their trainin's all wrong. When they've been runnin' round 'ere all week, they're that damned dizzy they don't know which way they're playin' or whose side they're on nor nowt ... Does tha support a team, nip?'

'Only a winning one.'

'Tha does reight. Ah only follow football i' winter, tha knows. Cricket's mi real sport. Cracked on it as a kid Ah were; allus thinkin' abhat ' willow an' ' leather.'

'Who did they play for?' Barney asked.

'Ah'm talkin' abaht ' bloody bat an' ball, comic!' Jake yelled at him. 'Ah wanted to be a professional when Ah grew up; play for Yorkshire, tha knows.'

'What stopped you?'

'Eleven others. An' bi ' time Ah were seventeen, like, mi eyes wouldn't focus proper. It got so as Ah only knew 'e'd bowled when Ah 'eard ' crack on mi stumps. Ah can't read print now baht specs.'

'Where are they?'

'Nivver 'ad any.'

'Well, surely it can't be that bad, then ... And what about your driving? You must have passed the reading test to get your licence.'

'Well, Ah knew it'd be ' first question 'e'd ask me as soon as we got i' ' car, so Ah memorized ' number plate o' ' one stood i' front. Ah can see reight enough, though. When Ah 'ave run into summat, Ah've generally recognized what it is.'

It was a scorching afternoon, and the heavy heat lay on us almost pinning us to the ground, but eventually Jake suggested that the address with the entry 'remove furniture' on the worksheet might provide us with something to add to the day's collection of scrap, and in less than ten minutes we drew up in the common yard at the back of the house, which was part of a long terrace. It was a dirty backwater with grey rags which passed for clothes suspended over the stony ground, and bloated women in sagging, printed dresses oozing over the back steps, their scruffy children yelling and laughing in and out of the shadows and the air reeking with the stench of overboiled cabbage. Sure enough, though, there was an iron bedstead with brass trimmings propped against the upstairs window, and Barney was hopping around like a jumping bean in his anxiety to convert it into a few coppers. Nobody answered when I knocked and as the place was not locked we went in. I had reached the middle of the room before realizing I was still holding the door and the hinges were swinging from the crumbling frame. There was a foot of water in the sink which had become green with plant life. The walls were wet and peeling and screwed-up bundles of dirty newspaper littered every nook and cranny. At first, it seemed that the floor was covered from wall to wall with white linoleum, but as we stood there taking it all in, the surface broke into a deep, moving ocean of fly-grubs, and black clouds of their parents rose in noisy anger and swarmed about our heads.

'Come aht on it,' Barney ordered from the doorway. 'We're not bahn in there till ' bug man's been. Them flies's big enough to be bloody man-eaters.'

'It's a bloody disgrace, that 'ole,' one of the women shouted. 'There's cockroaches from there gettin' under ' skirtin' boards in our 'ouse. There ought to be a bloody law against it.'

'Bloody disgrace!' echoed the toddler on her knee.

A small, slightly-built man with a nervous grin and eyes that wandered over your shoulder when he spoke to you sidled towards us.

'No sign of life there?' he asked.

'I wouldn't say that, but there's nobody in.'

'Ah don't suppose when yer've done there, yer could move a few slates from my 'ouse, could yer?'

'We're not allowed to. We can only do what they gie us on this 'ere sheet.'

'Aye! Well! Ah just wondered, like. Ah didn't know yer 'ad them rules, else Ah wouldn't 'ave asked ... Ah mean it's not ' sort o' day yer want to be doin' more na yer're forced.'

'It's a warm un, all reight.'

'Nay, Ah shouldn't like your job i' weather like this. Yer mun be fair roastin' ... Would yer all like a drink?'

9 Sparky

'Tha wants to watch 'im or 'e'll be 'avin' forty winks i' t' street. An' whatever tha does, don't let 'im get 'is brush 'andle under 'is chin, 'cos when 'e does that, 'e's fast on i' ' middle o' ' causeway.'

The subject of this warning was one Cuthbert Haste, a roadsweeper who worked in the town centre. His regular companion had gone down with a chest infection and I was taking his place. Cuthbert was about thirty, a small, dumpy figure with a smooth, round face and wisps of hair that, having survived the ravages of alopecia, floated round his head like so many dandelion seeds. To hide his baldness, he wore a large, checked, flat cap which never altered its position from day to day, and everyone suspected he had glued it on. His eyelids drooped drowsily, so that only the bottom half of his pupils ever peeped underneath and he looked to be in a permanent stupor. As if that were not enough to keep Nature in stitches, he had come into the world with no roof in his mouth, and any conversation with him generally left you wondering what it was about, while the face of a lost motorist listening to Cuthbert giving directions — and then changing them — for ten minutes bore expression beyond description.

''E'd go to sleep 'angin' off a cliff edge, yon. Does tha know, 'is mate says they were 'avin' their snap in this café i' ' Arcade, an' 'e gets this teacake aht an' takes one bite an' goes to sleep for five minutes just sat like that wi' a ruddy great teacake stickin' aht on 'is gob.'

As it happened, it was Cuthbert Haste who woke me up. We had trundled the barrow as far as the bus station, and as it was about half-past-seven by then — just an hour before snap-time — he had disappeared for his breakfast. It was market day, and I sat on one of the empty stalls to watch May Day Green erupt into bustling activity as canvas roofs slipped over the wooden frameworks, vans and lorries rumbled in and out of the confusion discharging their sundry and exotic cargoes, towers of wicker baskets swayed against the sturdy props and the boards creaked and sagged beneath a welter of fruits and vegetables, carpets, fish, potted plants and flowers, duffle jackets or children's toys. The noise of the engines and the swearing and the shouting grew ever more faint, and the next thing I remembered was a broom handle rudely butting into my navel with the punch of a small battering-ram. It was half-past-ten.

'Ar ... oure ... oo ... som ... ah,' said Cuthbert.

'Pardon?'

After several similar deathless exchanges and a few useful gestures it became clear to me that we were about to plunge headlong into our morning duties. Seeing that he had now convinced me, Cuthbert assumed charge of the barrow, and we idled in silence up Queen's Road. There was a great deal of excavation going on at the west side of the market where, deep down, they were laying a chain of large, concrete pipes. For some minutes we stood by this hole and looked over the work in progress with a critical eye.

'Wau ... mob ... sa ... reri ... o,' Cuthbert shouted down to them with a laugh.

Two navvies glanced at each other.

'Eh?'

That settled, we turned around the block and along Eldon Street. The shops were not yet open, and their dark emptiness, and the tall, wooden gates across the entrances made them look lost and drab even in that bright morning light. On the upper storeys, the vacant offices were screened by rows of smoky panes of glass which pitted the soot-crusted stone facades and the fancy gables as they rose in shabby elegance into the skies. Down the street as far as we could see there was litter spattered in the gutters and on the pavements as thickly as the autumn leaves, and there appeared to be enough to occupy two teams for days. But Cuthbert walked on through it all as though there was not a piece of waste-paper in sight.

'Aren't we going to sweep this then?'

'What day is it today?' he seemed to be saying.

'Wednesday.'

'We don't clean 'ere till Friday.'

'But it's dirty now.'

'Ah don't care. Folks should learn to throw their muck away o' Thursdays.'

It was only in Midland Street that he finally rested the barrow. At the far end was the stall where I had been sitting not so long ago: we had walked in almost a complete circle.

'Do we clean this road on Wednesdays?'

'We clean this every day. ' Fox comes back to work along this part o' mi rounds after 'is dinner. We 'ave this lookin' like a new pin, choose 'ow mucky ' rest is.'

Nonetheless, we had only swept halfway down one side of the street — a good thirty yards — when he decided it was time for dinner. The consequences were remarkable. All his good intentions seemed to evaporate instantly in the necessity of the moment: he had not even time to tuck the barrow out of the way, but leaving it just as it was in the gutter, he set off home with the very helpful suggestion thrown over his shoulder to me that I should come back when he did. It was half-past-eleven, and we had been working for exactly fourteen minutes. I mentioned this to Jake when I saw him in the canteen, but he seemed unimpressed.

"E's just a bit simple, nip ... but 'e'll be sharp enough not to get caught. 'E were once takin' 'is barrow down ' middle o' Market Street in ' wrong direction, an' this bobby pulls 'im up an' says, "Where's tha think tha're goin': this's a one-way street," an' Cuthbert says to 'im, "Wuh, Ah'm only goin' one way". Now what could t' old bobby do but let 'im off?'

Cuthbert returned to his post sometime after two o'clock, reeking of pickled onions and belching with unashamed vigour, which frightened the life out of passing shoppers. In the first half-hour he sat on the barrow, saying nothing and eyeing the passers-by with casual interest. Finally, he gave a great yawn, stretched his short limbs, produced a belch like the Crack of Doom and we settled down to sweeping Midland Street again — not that end that was as yet virgin soil, but the part which we had already done. As the effects of our morning's effort had still not worn off, the repeat performance took only twelve minutes. Again, once we had dealt with that particular stretch, Cuthbert wandered off up the Arcade — this time with the barrow — and without a word of explanation. There was a narrow alleyway a little to the left of the cinema, and after a quick scout round for unwelcome eyes we slipped along its secret crannies. Someone was already there, Hoyland, who swept around the Town Hall, perhaps out of a sense of nostalgia, for in happier days he had once stood for Parliament in Lincolnshire. As we found him he was sitting with his back against the wheel of his barrow and a flask of tea at his side, studying the pages of some girlie magazines he had picked out of a litter bin.

'Aza ... goc ... eeo ... urg ... ou,' he greeted us, his face contorted like a grotesque mark as he struggled to overcome his impediment.

The gist of his introduction appeared to be that he had every sympathy for me being the poor bugger having to work with Cuthbert, who drove everybody up the wall because no-one could understand a word he said. The situation hardly lent itself to any tactful form of reply. So, I resigned myself to a seat on a dustbin lid, listening to the two of them gargling away to each other all afternoon. What they were talking about I had no idea, but by the time we left for the yard I was completely satisfied that Hoyland would, in the event, have been no less at home in the House of Commons.

Many more days like that and I would have noticed everyone to whom I spoke looking blankly at me and asking if I would repeat myelf, but on the following morning Gabby dragged Chris into the inspector's office and poked Mike O'Grady in the chest. Gabby, who saw himself as the senior sweeper in his crew, was by far the smallest member on the force — he had not improved in stature by growing bowlegs — and as he stood there he was just about as tall as Chris's trousers. So, it was no mean feat that he poked Mike in the ribs, and perhaps gave some indication of how upset he was.

'Now look 'ere, Mike,' he began. 'Where's ' sense i' puttin' a beanstalk like this to work wi' some one like me? Ah've dislocated mi neck tryin' to shout up to 'im, an' Ah can't 'ear a damn word 'e says.'

'Well, what's wrong with him, Gabby?' Mike asked. 'He seems a nice young lad ... and I should have thought you couldn't afford to lose him: he must be doing most of the work on your round because he's obviously out in the open more often — he's the only one with a suntan ...'

'Arr! 'e got that while it were chuckin' it down on every other bugger in Barnsley. Nay, we want someone who knew when to stop growin'. Ah'm 'avin' to jump aht o' ' road every time 'e passes i' case 'e steps on mi. An' Ah'll swear 'e grows three feet every time it rains.'

It was raining that day when Mike sent me to join Gabby's crew in place of Chris. Dark clouds shadowed the already dark hills of Barnsley and rows of dull brick and grey slate stood dejected and bedraggled against the sullen sky. The pavements were swallowed up by enormous puddles, while faceless people, smothered in high collars and shawls, splashed through them and swore volubly.

The four of us, Gabby, Smithy, Roper and I, were ranged on chairs around the caretaker's room at the school at the bottom of the hill. The chairs were small, because it was a junior school and only Gabby was sitting comfortably, but the little room was nicely heated — although it was the fifth week of the summer holidays — by the school boiler which stood in the centre, and we were all drinking mugs of school tea.

'Thank God yer don't bring yon Ben wi' yer anymore,' said Sam, the caretaker. 'It weren't that Ah minded 'im comin' in aht o' ' rain wi' yer all; it were 'im draggin' yon great barrow in after 'im as got me.'

'Was he so attached to his work?' I asked.

'Nay, it weren't ' barrow as worried Sam 'ere,' Gabby said. 'It used to be them sacks 'e 'ad on ' back wi' all t' stuff 'e'd picked up from ' road, an' 'e'd bring 'em in to keep 'em dry. Arr, 'e were reight mean tha knows: nivver missed a trick. 'E could see a tanner i' ' gutter thirty yards off. Nivver let owt pass 'im. Meanest man Ah ever knew ... Does tha know, when 'is wife'd cut 'er toenails, 'e used to pick up ' bits an' put 'em on 'is compost ... It's reight. Any'ow, if 'e used to find a piece o' coke i' ' road 'e'd put it i' one o' these sacks; or if 'e fun some coal, that'd go in another sack. 'E'd got sacks for everythin' ... 'E even 'ad one for 'orse-muck. An' if 'e saw a 'orse i' street, 'e'd stop ' job altogether, an' tha'd see 'im runnin' up ' road after it wi' a shovel in one 'and an' 'is sack i' t' other shoutin' "Shit, yer bugger, Shit!". Ooo, that were ' worst, if 'e got that bag nearest ' fire. Used to 'afe suffocate us, didn't it Sam?'

Sam and he shook their heads sadly at the memory. Gabby, in

spite of his size, was the well-oiled mouthpiece of the crew, and Roper and Smithy had to be content to sit for long periods in the shades of silence. In fact, Roper had very little to do with the rest, and always sat as much away from us as possible. In the utmost confidence, he once told me that, when he had come down from Cumberland, this was the only job he could find but he was constantly looking for other employment, so that at least he could work with some decent people. He was a strict Methodist, who neither smoked nor drank, and was fortified to find that, as the Scriptures said, Life was but a trial. He had set his sights on a Heaven which provided a very superior accommodation, and even if the real thing turned out to be not quite so grand as the brochures described it, he was certainly not going to be satisfied with one that would lower its standards to admit dustmen.

'It used to worry mi every time 'e brought them sacks in, i' case someone fun aht,' Sam continued. 'Last time 'e did it, ' fumes got into ' classroom above, an' ' 'eadmaster 'ad 'em all aht i' ' playground checkin' to see who'd messed 'is breeches.'

'Poor sods!' said Smithy.

'Ah'm not so sure, though: tha nivver knows wi' kids,' Sam said. 'They're warm uns these days. Does tha know, there's young uns 'ere go climbin' over ' cubicle walls i' ' bogs an' lockin' all doors on ' inside ... girls an' all. Every week, it 'appens. Then there's poor little buggers shittin' theirsens 'cos they can't get in ... An' some on 'em as a mucky trick o' wipin' their arses on ' bog roll baht tearin' it off an' then rollin' it back for ' next un to find.'

The rain had stopped by now, but the sky still brooded sulkily, so we took a slow leave of the dusty boiler-room and its cosy warmth. Just as we had resigned ourselves to the misery of wading all day through the waterchoked gutters, however, the electric cart decided it had seen enough for one morning and refused to respond. We tried all the normal, recognized procedures for correcting the fault, such as kicking it, switching the leads and putting rainwater in the batteries. But our efforts came to nothing and the only remaining course of action was to telephone the depot — on a reverse-charge call, of course — and report the breakdown. About an hour later, we did just that.

It was Gabby who suggested that we push the cart on to the road in case the Superintendent came along to inquire what it was doing underneath the school bicycle-shed, although Gabby felt unable to lend his shoulder as he had once broken it. It was Gabby who thought we should empty the garbage into the yard of a pub on Wakefield Road before the cart was towed away, but somehow his turn with the shovel never seemed to come. And it was Gabby who told the mechanic how to secure the rope to the cart as we sat in the back of the breakdown lorry. He was telling us how his wife had mistakenly used his gall-stones, which he kept in a jar, to make piccalilli and how his sister-in-law had broken one of her teeth on them when, almost on the summit of Harborough Hills Road, the rope snapped, and the cart began to roll back the way it had come. We all gave chase — except Gabby — but it was in vain, for, after running between a woman and the pram she was pushing across the road, it crashed through a garden wall and caused havoc in the sweet-pea bed. Gabby was furious at our slowness: he happened to live there.

Next day was fine and we lay all morning tucked out of sight on a rocky outcrop above Wakefield Road, with the new cart hidden under the ledge. Gabby was in full flight with a never-ending reel of stories; about how he had been summonsed to appear in court for something he knew nothing about, how he had sweated before they realized the summons had been wrongly addressed, and how annoyed he had been, although had they mentioned certain other matters which had arisen about that time he would have seen the force of their argument. On another occasion, when he had been working down the pit, his daughter had packed up his sandwiches and put the crust slivers in a paper bag which he had taken by mistake, and when the pit-manager had seen them he thought he had found the reason why Gabby was so small and fed him right royally at the company's expense for a week. The morning sped by for him, while the rest of us basked in the welcome sunshine and Roper browsed through a pocket bible.

'It pays to be small, sometimes,' Gabby waxed. 'Ah remember seein' ' rentman comin' once an' we'd nowt i' ' kitty 'cos Ah'd just put mi wages on a dog. So Ah rolled mi trousers up an' 'idded mi face be'ind a comic, an' when 'e opens ' door, 'e shouts, "Tha're six month owin': where's thi mam?", Ah squeaks, "She's gone aht".'

'Ah've allus liked Thursdays,' said Smithy.

He pulled his false teeth out of his jacket pocket and wiped off a few pieces of fluff before fitting them in so that he could savage the sandwich he had saved from his snap.

'Ah were nearly thirty before Ah 'ad to pay full-fare on ' bus,' added Gabby.

'Mind, it's pay day. That 'elps. But Ah've allus liked Thursday. It were even better when Ah were wi' ' Poggy crew. Randy Steve used to be touchin' this young bird up on Thursdays an' she used to let us i' ' kitchen an' leave us ' biscuit tin while them two went upstairs.'

'It must have looked a bit odd to the neighbours, though, a queue of men using her kitchen as a waiting-room while she took them on by appointment.'

'Well, 'er old man nivver got to know, any'ow. Ah used to see 'im down at ' pub, an' 'e nivver batted an eyelid. Mind, 'e used to go on summat terrible abaht ' way she got through packets o' biscuits.'

As the searing sun soared to its zenith we decided to postpone our rest until after the mid-day break. We gathered on the footpath back to the road, while Smithy went down to collect the cart.

'Damn!' he snapped, his finger flicking the operating button. 'It won't shift.'

'Damn!' said Gabby. 'We're bahn to 'ave to push it.'

'An' on a Thursday an' all.'

There were hardly any carts in working order on the next day. A gang of teenagers had broken into the docking shed and disconnected them all from the recharging unit, so that most of the batteries were flat. Gabby, Roper and Smithy were reduced to taking out a hand-cart, and I was sent to make up the numbers on the electric dustlorry. This was just a bigger version of the ordinary electric dustcart, with the decided advantage of having seating accommodation. The cabin was intended to fit a crew of five, but someone had forgotten to mention Big Jim to the designer. Big Jim was enormous, and when he sat on the long back seat, the lorry groaned as if the breath was being pressed out of it. He had the paunch of a pregnant elephant, and his overalls had to be made-to-measure, perhaps an unusual concession for his services, especially as he perspired so much that they rotted away at the rate of four pairs a year. His main pastime — in fact his only pastime — was drinking: it could really be described as an all-consuming passion. He boasted that he made a tour of all the pubs in Barnsley once a year, and if he did not fall flat on his face after fifteen pints the landlord must be tampering with the beer. His real problem, however, was that once he had fallen down, it took all the king's men to get him back on his feet and he could not do it himself, no matter how sober he was. So if one morning he failed to appear at the depot the first deed of the day was to send out a rescue-party to his home to see if he had keeled over while putting on his socks. It was as a result of Big Jim's condition that we always had to sweep uphill, because if he leaned over a shovel while contemplating the valley below he would not take long in getting to the bottom of it.

All this very much suited Cough the Czech. Cough was not his real name but it was as near as we could pronounce it. He was a wizened figure, lame in one leg, and he spent much of the day bending down for the undisguised purpose of looking up the skirts of passing girls, so the steeper the incline, the better. On the whole it was an unusual hobby to indulge in so openly, but he said quite bluntly that it beat train-spotting any day. Obviously he had absolutely no inhibitions whatsoever about his behaviour, so in view of his enthusiasm it seemed rather a pity that there were others who had. Time after time, he was reported for indecency, especially on those occasions when the contents of a particular girl's skirt moved him to bawl across to his workmates, in a very ungallant fashion, 'Nossing!' while his victim went scarlet with embarrassment. There was little point in complaining, however. Those who did had to repair their dignity with the understanding that, while he would, of course, be severely reprimanded, it would really be unfair to take further action as he was only offensive owing to his foreign upbringing; but the truth of the matter seemed to be that there was little scope for anything else, seeing that he had originally been sent road-sweeping as a punishment anyway. Before that he had been a binner but he had disgraced himself one day when he came across the bin of a house on the New Lodge estate choked with over forty unwashed milk bottles. The discovery had made his blood seethe with anger, and when the man drew back his bedroom curtains an hour or so later he found a message printed in empty milk bottles on his front lawn inviting him to 'PISS OFF'. Cough's explanation was that he was trying to stimulate the man's sense of responsibility towards his local Co-op, but Mr Priest, the then Superintendent, was well known for his disapproval of these one-man social crusades — especially from the working classes — and his immediate response was to send Cough to sweep the streets until his English improved. Since then, his vocabulary had grown by leaps and bounds, but regrettably it had remained of a rather personal nature, so while the obvious curb to his present investigations was to send him back on a dustbin round where he would not even have time to bend down to tie his bootlace, there was always the risk that, armed with sufficient milk bottles, he could now say something really upsetting. In any case, as he had been sweeping the streets undisturbed for five years to date, it seemed fairly certain that the authorities considered dealing with the shockwave which would follow the release of his awakened literary powers into the suburbs of Barnsley a much more menacing prospect — if less interesting — than listening to the problems of women who do not wear underclothes.

It had been an uneventful day by the time we left the working-men's club. None of us was a member — although at three o'clock, that must have been self-evident — so we had not been allowed to buy beer there. But the manager of the club was Big Jim's uncle, and during the two hours immediately after the mid-day break he had supplied us free of charge with unlimited quantities of a remarkably similar liquid called spillage. So it was that we were sitting in the hot cabin being slowly grilled and feeling muzzy-headed when a long, articulated lorry passed us. There seemed nothing particularly unusual about it until it went round the bend and one of its rear wheels carried straight on down a side street. Ginger switched on the motor at once — that is, after he had twice attempted to force the starting key into the control for the windscreen wipers — and gave chase. At first he was undecided whether to go after the lorry or the wheel and as he reached the junction his driving strongly suggested that he was attempting to do both. Just before we became part of the wall at the corner he shouted that he was going to warn the driver and set a steady course. It was a fanciful exercise, really, pursuing a speeding lorry in a vehicle that would only touch forty miles an hour if it was going downhill with the aid of a high wind, and we might have been chasing it still if the dustlorry had not suddenly bucked and shuddered in a violent bout of hiccoughs and crashed to a halt against the kerb. Big Jim put his head out of the rear window and scanned the roadway behind us.

'Some stupid bugger's left a battery lyin' i' middle o' ' road,' he bawled.

Ginger followed the line of his pointing finger.

'Arr!' he said. 'It's ours.'

One morning, not long afterwards, I was sitting in the inspector's office watching Mike make out the timesheets, when the figure of Cuthbert Haste appeared in the doorway tightly gripping a brush as though he meant business.

'Ah say, Mike,' he gurgled, choking over each word, 'Ah want someone to work wi' today. Ah'm not workin' on mi own no more.'

'Can't be done, Cuthbert. Anyhow, word has it you don't work when you've got someone with you.'

'Ah'm tellin' thee Ah'm not workin' if there's just one o' mi.'

'To be honest, Cuthbert, I'm not sure Barnsley is ready yet for any more. You know what they say; more haste, less speed. If you want someone else, though, take this young lad.'

Cuthbert looked at me, and for once his sleepy eyes flashed with horror.

'Take 'im? No fear! Ah've 'eard on 'im; they say 'e's electric. 'E's only to come four feet from a barrow an' it blows a fuse or falls to bits. "Sparky", they're callin' 'im round 'ere. Nay, Ah'll work on mi own if that's all tha's got, but Ah'm warnin' thee if tha puts 'im anywhere near mi Ah'm off 'ome.'

10 The House

The old man died on the way back from the fish-and-chip shop. Mike O'Grady, the inspector, found him lying on a heap of rubbish just inside the entrance to the Cleansing Department with his head in a puddle and the rain pelting his withered form. His beard was a week old, his clothes stiff and stale, and his sole personal effects were a watch chain and a packet of soggy chips. Some knew him, vaguely, as Ron, others as Bob. But the truth was no-one had had very much to do with him. He had been in the army all his working life, and retired on a sergeant's pension. Since his father died over twenty years ago he had lived alone in a house in Oakwell Terrace, and rarely went out except when the fish-and-chip shop was open. He had never married, had no relatives and no friends. I never saw him, but Mike said when he looked down at that careworn, lonely face he could have wept. It is not everybody's way of dying, but with no-one to be responsible for the funeral arrangements, there was general approval in the canteen of his thoughtfulness in expiring where he did.

Jake was on holiday that week and Paul, his replacement, after just two unforgettable days, had proved his driving to be the finest inspiration to prayer since John Wesley's sermons. Our journeys through Barnsley were invariably marked by a display of acrobatics from pedestrians and drivers alike which would have daunted the most daring of trapeze artistes, while Barney and I had more than once climbed out of the wagon in such a nervous condition that the Arctic winds might have been rattling our bones. There was no doubt about it, whatever faults Paul had, he made life interesting, if short.

Our first visit on the Wednesday morning was to the back yard of a prominent firm of solicitors. The worksheet abruptly instructed us to 'remove hedge clippings', but the piles of vegetation that we found there must once have formed a substantial area of Sherwood

Forest. Barney was all for setting fire to it before anyone came on the scene — it was not quite eight o'clock — but was eventually persuaded to get out and guide Paul as he backed the wagon into the drive. There was a pair of beautiful, wrought-iron gates across the entrance, but even when opened to their widest, they gave little room for manoeuvre.

'Left!' Barney shouted. 'Reight! Straighten up! Watch thi mirror! Watch thi ...'

Crash! Paul's right wing-mirror disappeared in a shower of splinters.

'That's a pity,' said Paul, quietly, and drove out again to correct his approach.

'Come on!' Barney shouted. 'Left! Ovver to ' left! Watch thi ...'

Crash!

'Oh crikey!' said Paul. 'That's fourteen years' bad luck. Ah'll be forty-three now afore Ah can 'ave a bit o' stray i' safety.'

'Straighten up!' Barney shouted as Paul made his third attempt. 'Come ovver! Whoa! Whoa! ...'

Crunch! There was a sickening jolt and I looked round just in time to see the crumpled gate being wrenched from its hinges and the ornate headstone toppling from its post, and dashing itself to pieces on the pavement.

'Bloody 'Ell fire!' said Paul.

Barney leapt into the cab beside me.

'Let's bugger off afore anyone sees us!' he ordered.

Like a bat out of Hell the lorry raced over the road and down the hill. We had almost reached the bottom when, to our utter dismay, Mike's grubby little van nipped round us and a sinewy arm shot out from it and flagged us to a halt. He must have witnessed the whole blundering episode. Every drop of blood we possessed drained into the seat as he walked back to us.

'You remember that old man from Oakwell Terrace dying on me a few weeks ago?' he said. 'Can you clear his house, out when you've got a minute? It's all to go on the tip.'

You could have powered a windmill with our sighs of relief. At that moment we would have taken on the entire row in half the time. But, somehow, enthusiasm soon waned, and before the van had rolled around the bend we were on our way to a betting shop that Paul knew opened early to back the favourite in the first race of the day at Chepstow. We never went back to the solicitors' in spite of a torrent of eloquent pleas and stormy threats from that quarter, but if it is any consolation to them, the horse came last.

We did not see Mike again until well into the afternoon as we came up out of Fitzwilliam Street, a steep, narrow road pointing towards the Town Hall. One of the barmaids was sitting on the back steps of the 'Fitzwilliam' pub sunning her thighs, and from the instant Paul clapped eyes on her his head was straining through the passenger's window to take full advantage of the weather. Left to its own devices, the lorry immediately switched to the continental drive-on-the-right, and a Bentley, whose driver had a very worried look on his face, all but pirouetted past us on our left.

'Didn't you see that car?' asked Mike, as we paused at the junction.

'What car?' Paul said, truly surprised.

Mike shook his head and sighed.

'Go down to Oakwell Terrace and clear that house out. And if you're going through town, for God's sake try not to look as if you're being driven by The Invisible Man.'

The house stood in a brick terrace just off Pontefract Road, only a minute's walk away from the yard entrance where the old man had collapsed. It was like stepping back into the past, coming into that street: the road was still paved with rust-brown cobble-stones and there were the old gas lamp-posts on the kerb edge and tubby men walking about in braces and collarless shirts. The air was warm, breathing a faint sweet smell like that of cut grass, and mellowing the drab russet walls and the uneven paving stones with a film of drowsy nostalgia. We pressed against the front window, our hands cupped over our eyes, trying to pierce the inner gloom. The pane was thick with grime, and ancient cotton curtains were draped across like dense cobwebs.

'Doesn't seem to 'ave whittled his pension away on soap, does 'e?' Paul remarked.

'Ah bet yon spent nowt on nowt,' Barney replied. ''E'll be one o' them blokes who stuffs 'is mattress full o' fivers. Let's get in an' make ussens rich.'

But even the grim exterior could not have prepared us for the wretchedness within. It was like walking into a world of quiet greyness: everywhere was grey, a layer of dust quarter of an inch deep on the sideboard, on the table, the cupboard shelves, the coat hung on the door, the floor, like a fall of grey, grey snow. Long, grey wisps festooned themselves around the walls whose patterned paper had long since faded behind a dark greenness, and the fireplace was choked with soot. There was a large armchair, its innards bulging from tears in its rotten fabric, with ghastly black patches over its arms and headrest. His jacket and trousers were flung across a chair in a crumpled heap, dirty and damp. A room without a soul save for the few glass ornaments and a stilled clock on the sideboard, and a rust-stained mirror over the fireplace. And from it all, in that heavy, gloomy silence arose the strong, nauseating smell of a man waning and decaying.

The scene in the kitchen was no less depressing. The paint was flaking even to the ceiling, and the damp had spread chains of festering mould from door to window. A tiny, filthy gas-cooker huddled in the darkest corner, daubed with huge wads of black grease. On the draining board was a packet of rancid butter and some sour milk. Everywhere else, from the floor to the cracked sink, lay strewn a jumbled mass of greasy newspapers littered with cold chips and shreds of stale fish, the crumpled remains of what must have been many unlovely and lonely meals. As we stood in the doorway and as the world flooded into this dimly-lit, crumbling tomb the papers rustled slightly and went limp. And then you could feel his stifled aching.

Barney was having a field day. In his mind's eye he had already converted the sideboard into a tool chest for his garden hut, and he had definite plans for the table. We had hardly noticed Paul gingerly going up the stairs which led off from the kitchen, but the revolted horror of the yell from the landing soon made amends, and after setting what must have been a new world-record time in descending a staircase, he tumbled into the kitchen choking and retching behind a handkerchief the sight of which would itself have left most people feeling extremely queasy.

'What's up?' Barney inquired.

.Paul, who was now well on the way to becoming the first green Englishman, could not answer him, however. Finally, Barney lost his patience, scoffed at the state of Paul's liver, and intrepidly climbed the stairs.

'Christ Jesus!'

Knocking seconds off Paul's athletic triumph he tumbled into the room in much the same condition.

'Just go up there, nip,' he invited me, before collapsing into a fit of spluttering. 'Go an' look! Jesus!'

The opportunity sounded like an agnostic's dream, yet on the whole I was inclined to doubt Barney's powers of identification, not only because at times he could not even recognize his workmates, but also because no-one in that situation would risk the insult of gripping his nostrils and running for it, no matter how bad the smell was. Moreover, Barney kept goats — goats whose body odour would have felled even another goat — so I was confident that any stench which could turn his stomach into heaving tripe would probably dissolve mine. My sense of adventure thus reduced to a whimper, I contented myself to suppose that if ignorance was not exactly bliss, it was undoubtedly preferable.

'Come on,' said Barney, reaching for the front door as if salvation lay on the other side. 'We can't do nowt now. We'll leave it till tomorrow.'

'Tha don't 'ave to be a mind reader to know what 'e's thinkin'.' Paul told me in an aside. 'Ah bet thee owt Barney don't turn up for work tomorrow.'

Barney did not turn up for work the following day. We went round in the spare wagon to call for him, but his sister informed us that his cold was too bad for him to see visitors — unless we happened to be the doctor. Not that Paul was able to brag about his foresight: he did not turn up either. Nevertheless, rumours had spread quickly through the depot, and although half-a-dozen men were available there was a rare lack of enthusiasm for manning the spare wagon that morning.

'You don't know you're born,' Mike scolded us. 'It's only a smell. When I was in Swansea we had to clean out a house where the bloke had died under the table and left his gas fire on in the middle of summer. He'd been there that many weeks he'd exploded and shot himself all over the room. Nobody knew he'd gone even until someone saw maggots crawling under the door. You never saw such a mess. There were bits of him everywhere, over chairs, on his bookshelves, in the sugar bowl, hanging from the lampshade. He'd even got into the television. I'll bet he was sixteen stones if he was a pound, there was that much of him. The undertaker left most of him as it was. In the end we got that tired of it we pushed what was left down the waste disposal unit. And talk about smell: you could hardly stand up in it. You've got it soft compared with us then.'

But no matter how hard Mike tried, we remained, on the whole, unconvinced by our apparent good fortune. Although the wagon's worksheet only required a crew of two, no-one would volunteer. Finally, by way of compromise, Mike sent all six of us there. Our protests were in vain, even after Chris had shrunk two inches from shock, for in less than a minute he had driven us out of the depot and we were walking down to Oakwell Terrace with everybody in a hurry to be at the back of the queue.

That momentary intrusion of yesterday had done nothing to freshen up the place. The air was still musty and oppressive; the greyness seemed greyer, and the room seemed burdened with a sense of weariness and overwhelming sadness. We wasted no ceremony on stripping the ground floor of its furniture. Without the aid of Barney's discriminating eye we packed it all on to the back of the wagon and let the totters on Lundwood tip boil with glee at the blessings of Providence. In less than twenty-five minutes everything on the ground floor was taken out and stowed on board the lorry. The whole street came out to watch, drawn by a neighbourly interest in another's privacy, and soon at least a dozen of them had brought stools out on to the pavement or had perched themselves on the doorstep with mugs of coffee and piles of biscuits, so as to miss nothing.

But disagreeable though the operation had been so far, it was no preparation for what was to follow.

The smell hit you as you reached the top of the stairs — hit you, like a physical blow, with such force that you were reeling over the banister and your head was swimming in a growing blackness. Nothing can accurately describe its inhuman vileness: it came from the cauldrons of Hell and you could only suppose that someone up there was boiling thousands of bad eggs in a vat of ammonia and spicing them with fishmeal and silage. For what seemed hours the well of the stairs rang with a confusion of suffocated swearing and full-blooded retching. It was no wonder the plaster was crumbling and the felt on the landing had been worn away into holes and masses of fluff: nothing could have survived for long in so poisonous an atmosphere.

Finally, Basil rather bravely pushed back the door to the rear bedroom with the intention of opening the window either by levering it or by jumping through it. But there was no need. There was not a single pane of glass in the window. It was a completely empty room — presumably evacuated when the ventilation got out of hand — bare to the floorboards and empty of fittings save for a crooked and rusty gas bracket on the far wall. Just how long it had lain in this dilapidated condition we could only guess, but it was certainly the ideal apartment for the unwelcome guest. The floor was strewn with slivers of glass and oases of grass and mosses: indeed there was so much soil accumulated there that had the old man ever had reason to venture in he could have turned it into a greenhouse in twenty minutes. Fungus spilled over the window sill and decorated the outer wall in broad streams, while toadstools and mushrooms had scattered to the four corners. A dark stain spreading from beneath the window told the story of many, heavy rainfalls over the years and the floorboards had rotted away just under the ledge, leaving a black hole staring like a great eye through the mildew.

'God Almighty!' said Basil.

In the circumstances, everybody seemed broadly to agree with him.

But though the room was powerfully fusty it was not responsible for that asphyxiating stench which was fast turning the entire company the colour of animated cabbages. The implications were obvious, and we hung about the open, back doorway not because the scene inspired our souls with heavenly beauty but because no-one could find any sense in being first to enter the other bedroom. The door across the landing was very slightly ajar, and breathing in so confined a space was becoming difficult, if not desirable, yet for a while eyes glanced at the opening as though it were a mirage. Then, somebody — who has probably regretted doing so ever since — slowly pushed open the door with his boot.

Silence met silence.

Outside the sun was shining out of a clear, summer-blue sky. The familiar sounds of a friendly world bounced happily across the streets and over the rooftops. Sparrows hopped along the gutter and chirped applause to the song of the thrush. The low drone of traffic on Pontefract Road. The thrilled shrieks of children playing out their games. Someone was praising the quality of supermarket cheese while a pram squeaked apologies to its slumbering charge as it came up the hill.

How many such days, filled with bright warm hours, had flitted away into the past while an old man lay up here hemmed in by a cage of creeping twilight and lonely eyes wandered endlessly from wall to wall? This place did not lie in the land of the living. There was something weird and unearthly about it; something that was utterly beyond the reach of human understanding. Everything was cast in darkness; not just ordinary darkness, but a darkness that was sullen and unpleasant, as though, while long year had crawled after long year, the miserable eternity of emptiness and unutterable longings in his unloved soul had spread a web of dreadful shadows to smother the room with repulsive ghastliness. Only the feeblest light could filter through, though the curtains, black as soot, stood drawn back like cloaks of mourning. Even the children's laughter in the street below seemed far removed and somehow unreal. The wallpaper hung in shreds stained with the hues of age, hideous greens and browns smeared with grime, the ceiling grey and brooding as the darkest thunder clouds. His wardrobe and dressing-table pressed themselves into the corners like gloomy phantoms in shrouds of dust: his bed lay unmade behind the door, the sheets worn through and gone so yellow and black you felt sick just to see them.

But by far the most curious feature of the room was the enormous quantity of bottles which crowded together in a broad fringe around the floor and on every flat surface from the window sill to the top of the wardrobe. There were hundreds of them everywhere, quart-sized lemonade bottles, not just side by side but lying on top of each other in the fashion of the most exclusive wine-vaults and three rows deep. At first glance, it seemed that the man had been overwhelmed by an extraordinary thirst in his last days, but when you realized, even through the half-light, that the bottles were still full to the brim, every one of them, the whole, awful truth began to dawn. There was enough urine there to account for every call Nature made upon him in ten years, stored away and now half-buried in the dust. And that was not all. Though the invention of lavatory paper had apparently not been disclosed to him, he had made abundant use of spare newspaper — presumably from the fish-and-chip shop — and crammed it in grubby layers in all the places he could find, under the bed, stuffed in every drawer, and from top to bottom of the wardrobe. Then, when there was no more room left and no more empty bottles he made free use of the floor, so that the carpet had almost disappeared, matted and caked in filth, and the walls were stained and smears and clots rose up the sides of the chest of drawers and spread over the bed, into the sheets and across the pillows. For up to twenty years he had lived in this home-made sewer and now had bequeathed enough concentrated fertilizer to supply the immediate needs of half the West Riding. And the poisonous air was so dense and sultry that you had to push your way in like wading through steaming porridge.

'I want to be sick,' wailed Chris.

'Well, go ahtside, then,' Basil ordered. 'We don't want thee muckyin' ' place up.'

'And while you're out,' Brian added, 'Go and ask Mike to come up here. I want to stitch his nose in this bedpost.'

'At least he had one good point. He must have been a strict teetotaller. There are only pop bottles here.'

'Damned good job, too,' Basil observed. 'Think 'ow many 'e'll 'ave taken back for 'is bottle money. It's put me off pop for life 'as this little lot. If Ah'd seen any beer bottles 'ere Ah'd 'ave dug 'im up an' strangled him, so 'elp me.'

'Well 'ow are be bahn to get it all on ' wagon?' said Harold, pointing to the wardrobe. 'Ah'm not walkin' down no stairs wi' that shit'ouse on mi back.'

Joe, the driver taking Paul's place, solved the problem. He brought the lorry on to the pavement against the wall and positioned it underneath the window. Six pairs of hands, in one urgent and desperate heave, pushed out the window frame, and we heard it shatter itself on the back of the wagon. Six heads leaned out of the gaping hole and gulped in wholesome air, bodies half-tumbling out like fledglings craning their necks to receive the first grub. I could see the faces of the neighbours on the opposite side grow hard with cold disapproval at this disgraceful display, but then, as the foul gases poured out into the open, first the nearest and then, in successive stages, those further away swept up their picnics and stools and slammed the doors behind them. For two hours as the house was being disembowelled the escaping odours stank out the street from one end to the other, and drove everybody inside, even the children, so that the place seemed like a decaying ghost-town. Bottles fell fast and furious out of the window until the spare wagon resembled a mobile swimming pool, and urine and filth slopped from its seams and ran down the pavement. Everything was dropped over the sill just as it stood, even the bed and the wardrobe, and the air rang with the sounds of glass splintering beneath them and the breadth of the street was showered with spray as they landed. Three loads the spare wagon took to the tip before the room was finally cleared out, and each time it went along Pontefract Road the doors and windows were shut tight in its wake, and passers-by were left rocking on their heels.

'Tha should 'ave seen them kids' faces on ' tip, yesterday,' grinned Joe, as we sat in the cab admiring the view from Carlton Hill on the following day. 'Tha knows 'ow they jump on ' wagon while it's still goin', an' tha can shout at 'em to get off till tha're blue i' ' face, them cheeky sods. Anyway they all jumped on ' first load, an' tha should 'ave seen 'em all go flyin' off again, all covered i' piss an' shit. They wouldn't go near ' wagon all day after that.'

'Smelt bad i' that room, did it?' asked Barney, with a grin on his face, having been called back to work from death's door just as the job was finished.

'Smell bad?!' Joe echoed. 'They were all aht paintin' red crosses on ' doors i' Oakwell Terrace, yesterday. By ' way, nip; what's tha done wi' that money tha fun?'

'What money?' Barney asked, his ears twitching.

'This lad fun five 'undred quid under ' lino in t' front room. We all knew 'e mun 'ave some tucked away somewhere, but 'e fun it an' kept quiet abaht it. 'E only told me 'cos Ah came in as 'e were pickin' it up.'

Barney missed the wink from Joe.

'Tha did reight, kid,' he said. 'If t'others 'ad 'eard on it, they'd all 'ave been greedy an' wanted some. Now if tha gies thissen a 'undred an' fifty each — 'cos tha did most o' work — an' me ' rest, we'll not tell that lot owt abaht it, eh?'

'But I've handed it in at the police station, already.'

'Tha're kiddin' me.'

'Nay, 'e's not, Barney.'

'What the 'Ell for? It's not their money.'

'It just seemed the proper thing to do.'

His face went pink, then white, then scarlet: his eyes gleamed on me like coals of fire and his body began to shake with fevers of rage. You could almost see the twisted frustration and the bitter regret at his untimely illness building up inside him.

'Proper thing to do?! Proper thing to do?! Tha damned, great, soft, bloody, stupid pillock! Tha're not fit to be let loose. Gie'in' five 'undred nicker away. Proper thing to do! Thee just wait. Ah'll show thee what ' proper thing to do is, kid.'

He felt behind the back of the seat and brought out a solid cylinder of steel, two feet long.

'What's that for?' I asked.

'Nivver thee mind. It's nowt to do wi' thee. Just thee 'old thi bloody 'ead still.'

11 Last Days

'Ee, look at that!' said Jake, approvingly.

We had come to the petrol station to remove a dead, stray cat that nobody wanted. It was only the third call of the day, yet the lorry was already quite full. We had stacked at the front the remains of a greenhouse which Barney had originally decided would be useful to him, in a way he thought best not to tell — although Jake and I had smashed most of it while being chased by a disagreeable alsatian, and that was why Barney was not speaking to us for the moment. Afterwards we had been into the yard of a pub on Wakefield Road to remove what appeared to be considerable quantities of road-sweepings which had been secretly dumped in front of the garage about a fortnight before, and had our ears singed into the bargain because the landlord in his fury had convinced himself that if we were not to blame for the inconvenience we ought to be. Even then we had room enough for a cat.

The garage was deserted as we drove into it, except for the petrol-pump attendant, a girl of about nineteen or twenty, who was sitting on the counter with her feet resting on the window ledge, and all she could see were the mountains where the heroine of her magazine had found her lover, rather than the more obvious slack-heap of a nearby Barnsley coal-mine. Our arrival seemed an intrusion beneath her attention and while the dashing, Swiss goat-herder swept her into his arms and whispered sweet nothings in Swiss into her pretty ear she leaned back and uninhibitedly stretched her legs, oblivious to us all. Drawn by the lure of her exposed thighs, Jake inched the spare wagon across the forecourt until we had a worm's eye view. And still she ignored us.

'Just look at that! Tha don't get many o' them to t' pound. An' she knows tha knows. But she's lovely. Ah could fair fancy that.'

The girl responded to his compliment by turning over a page.

'Corporation, love!' Jake shouted. 'Where's Pussy?'

She raised her head with undisguised disappointment. We did not look like Swiss goat-herders.

'Round ' back!' she yelled, and fled back up the Alpine path.

'There's a novelty,' replied Jake. 'Ah bet that's puzzled a few.'

Her gaze remained fixed to the page. Barney grunted, either in appreciation or disgust, and disappeared round the side carrying a shovel. Jake rested his head on the driving-wheel and followed the beckoning line of her leg. But she never moved.

'That's a lovely sight, i'nt it, nip?'

'It certainly puts the slack-heap in the shade.'

'She'd be just reight for thee, nice little piece like that. Tha wants to ask 'er aht.'

'If she's been sat like that all morning, I'm going to be a long way back in the queue.'

The girl put down her magazine and came out with a bucket and flannel as if she were about to wash down the pumps.

'Lovely! Lovely!' Jake applauded. 'Ah bet yer've got 'undreds o' boyfriends, nice girl like yawh.'

'Might 'ave.'

'Mi mate 'ere's wantin' a girl.'

She eyed me with withering criticism.

'Why?'

''E thought yer might like to get together toneet.'

'What for?'

''Cos 'e fancies yer.'

'Don't say much for 'issen, does 'e?'

''E don't 'ave to be good at talkin' an' all, does 'e?'

Just then Barney returned with the cat's remains, teeming with grubs and squashed so flat it looked like a miniature tiger-skin rug.

'Let's push off,' he suggested, climbing up beside us. 'Ah'm covered i' bugs from that bugger.'

'Nivver mind, nip,' said Jake, as he started the engine. 'We'll find one for thee somewhere.'

The next job on the list was to clear up a pile of ash somewhere in Worsborough Common, so we took the short cut across the housing estate. There was not a soul on the streets except a tall, slim girl with bobbing, black hair, who came out of a shop as we approached. Jake whistled, and she half-turned her head, then thought better of it and walked on.

'Ee, there's a nice little chassis there. Couldn't tha fancy that, nip?'

'Well, her face looks quite pretty from the back.'

'Nay, ' face 'as nowt to do wi' it. Tha're not watchin' ' mantelpiece when tha're pokin' ' fire.'

'Perhaps not; but they say you feel better if you know the brasses are polished.'

The lorry slowed down to a crawl and we followed the girl about ten yards behind while we discussed her more obvious and her potential merits. But in spite of the compliment, she was determined to show that as far as she was concerned we were not even there: she walked with her gaze fixed to the road ahead and the sway of her hips became slightly more pronounced, her body erect and just occasionally, the corner of her eye became visible.

'Mind, Ah felt like that when Ah were thy age,' said Jake. 'Ah used to look aht for a nice little figure. But tha wants to try it wi' a woman wi' some meat on. They're ' best, tha knows, fat women, wi' summat tha can get thi arms round. After that, a skinny bird does nowt for thee: it's like gettin' into bed wi' a rattlesnake.'

The girl never faltered, but her back was positively arched, and she tossed back her flowing mane with haughty contempt.

'Tha sees, a fat woman cushions thee while tha're on t' job. But when tha's finished wi' a bony bird, tha feels like 'er pelvis 'as ruptured thi gut. Besides, fat uns do it best 'cos they like it more. An' if tha gets 'em goin', they're fartin' away like 'ell 'cos they can't 'elp it. That's what tha listens for. An' when they're fartin' fit to blow thi legs off, there's nowt like it, Ah can tell thee.'

The girl had pushed open a garden gate and strutted down the path with deliberate coolness. But as she reached the front porch she turned, with a smile on her lips and a seductive glint in her eyes, and waved as she opened the door.

'Did tha see that?!' Jake gasped, as he jerked the wagon to a halt by the gate, and began taking off his jacket. 'Tha're in, nip. In fact Ah think we're all in.'

'That may be so,' I said, having a better view of the kitchen window, 'But so is her husband.'

The ash lay in the middle of the back yard of a long row of

terraced houses. We met considerable problems in getting to it as the Monday washing was strung out from end to end, and I had to lie on the cabin roof, carefully lifting lines of socks and string-vests over the headboard. There was no difficulty in recognizing it, however, a mound three feet high piled into a bay between two rows of lavatories and stinking like a ripe cheese fit to kill mice without the aid of a trap. The head had reduced it to a fine powder, and with scarcely half a dozen shovelsful on the wagon we were covered from head to foot in a crumbling coat of dark-brown dust.

'Ah didn't know as we 'ad niggers on ' Council,' yelled a fat old woman, tied up in a flowered pinafore and a scarf wrapped turban-style round her head; she giggled as she smoothed a rubbing-stone over the edge of the kitchen step.

'Why, 'an't tha ever seen dustmen afore?' Jake answered.

'Yer'll pem when yer've finished that.'

'Yer're not kiddin'. What is this muck? Dried goat?'

'Nowt to do wi' me. Next door's, that. Bloody stink it is, though. Us in this 'ere yard mun be ' only folk i' Barnsley who 'as to shut their toilet doors to keep ' smell aht.'

An upstairs window flew open suddenly, squealing with shock.

'Look what yer're doin' to mi weshin', yer clumsy idiots!'

We looked, and saw that we were, in fact, turning it a uniform shade of brown as great clouds of fine ash swept towards the far end of the yard. Like a string of frenzied cuckoo clocks back doors opened, and frantic housewives ran back and forth rushing armfuls of washing into their kitchens. The exception was the woman throwing a fit in her bedroom, for hers was the washing on the nearest line and those sheets were already the colour of stained oak.

'Look what yer've done to mi wesh, yer brainless buggers!'

'Don't take on so, 'Ilda,' cackled the crone on the steps. 'They've looked like that for years. It mun be that black fancy man you 'ad what rubbed 'is colour off on t' sheets.'

'Shut yer gob, yer ugly cow. At least Ah put mahn i' ' tub every week. Ah've not seen yours aht for so long Ah'm beginnin' to think yer don't 'ave none.'

'Nay, Ah don't 'ave to do mahn as often as yawh. My 'usband don't piss 'is sheets rotten every neet.'

'Don't 'e? From what 'e tells our Bernie, Sybil Walker, 'e pisses 'issen every time 'e looks at yer.'

Barney let out a very untimely guffaw. Hilda rounded on him at once.

'What's yawh laughin' at, yer ignorant bugger. That's two hours' work ruined. Ah've a good mind to drag yer all in bi ' ear an' make yer do it all again. What do yer think to that, now then?'

'Arse'ole!' thought Barney, without hesitation.

For a few moments Hilda just stared down at him not believing her own ears.

'Arse'ole?! Did yawh say "arse'ole" to me, yer bloody, foul-mouthed bugger? Ah've nivver been spoken to like that in all my life. Yer cheeky swine! Just yawh wait till Ah fetch mi 'usband aht 'ere. Ah'll teach yer to say "arse'ole" to me.'

She disappeared inside promising to return with her husband for a short coaching session in elocution.

'Tha's done it now,' Jake observed. 'Let's be off, quick!'

Throwing our shovels on to the back of the wagon we ran for the cabin. Jake had just started up the engine when a kind of gorilla in shirt-sleeves lumbered down the steps. Certainly he was the most effective-looking teaching aid I have ever seen, and Jake apparently thought so too, for with his foot hard on the accelerator, he sent the lorry screaming for the freedom of the open road. Ping, ping, ping went the washing lines as the wagon burst through them, and the screeches of Sybil and her friends were drowned by gales of laughter from Hilda and the others right to the far end.

For long enough afterwards, Barney found all sorts of excuses for us not visiting that quarter of town until calls turned into complaints and complaints into demands. In the end, Mike and the Fox almost frog-marched us there to deal with a pile of bricks that was pushing in the wall of a private garage. The lady of the house was in no better mood than Hilda. Service? Did we call this service? What on earth did she pay rates for and the dustbin had not been emptied for a fortnight either. None of us looked as though we knew what a decent day's work meant. We had no business being public servants: her father had been manager of a woollen mill before he died, and she was going to stand over us until every last brick had been picked up. Which she did, and a few weeks later we saw with some satisfaction that the wall had collapsed the other way.

But I did not see much more of Barney after that. A few days later we were travelling down Doncaster Road because along there was the job he had decided we should do next. He could not read, but being the ganger, he insisted on exercising his responsibilities, so Jake used to hold out the worksheet, and Barney would, by pointing with his finger, choose the order in which we went through it. It was a pointless practice, however, as Jake would then work down the list as he wanted with Barney none the wiser. In fact it left Barney at a considerable disadvantage for, if there was a chore which looked particularly unsavoury, Jake would simply ignore it for days and weeks on end until, eventually, Barney was hauled up before the Superintendent to explain why he was avoiding clear instructions. These interviews were evidently not at all pleasant, for Barney would emerge thoroughly bewildered and reduced to a gibbering, sweating jelly, but they served one useful purpose in that Jake would then know it was time to fall sick for a few days.

'This is it,' said Jake as we reached the cemetery.

Barney's face froze a deathly white.

'We're not bahn in 'ere, are we?'

'Arr! We 'ave to. It says "Collect box".'

'Box?' Barney rapped in alarm. 'What kind o' box?'

'It don't say,' said Jake, pulling up by the Chapel of Rest.

Trembling like a leaf, Barney opened the cabin door. Perhaps he then lost his balance, for, suddenly, he vanished, and when we leaned over to look for him, he was lying on the pavement nursing his famous, weak foot.

'Mi ankle! Mi ankle!' he kept repeating amongst other things.

'Gie o'er coddin' us!' Jake scoffed. 'There's nowt wrong wi' thi ankle. Tha're just tryin' to get aht o' doin' a job as usual.'

After all those years, it was no use trying to pull the wool over Jake's eyes. He knew his tricks too well. There was nothing wrong with Barney's ankle; he had only broken his leg. So, we took him to hospital, stretched out on the back of the wagon where his screams, as we rattled and jolted over the road, would not disturb us. When we left him he was being wheeled down to the X-ray room and he and a staff-nurse were having a violent argument about whether he was going to wear his flat cap in bed.

Everything seemed very quiet after he had gone. Fingers, who came in his place, was a different personality altogether, mild-mannered, gentle in his actions and with a voice like the whisper of a ghost. He acquired his nickname as a rather pointed observation that he now possessed less digits than the considered average, the discrepancy arising when, as a joiner's apprentice, he caught his sleeve in a circular saw and watched helplessly as his forefinger was gradually sliced off in rashers right up to the second joint. His other claim to originality lay in a pair of staring, bulbous eyes that almost hung out on stalks and might have been the symptoms of Bright's disease, but as the man himself said, when you have seen your finger slowly whittled down to a stub about an inch long, you are bound to come away looking a little bit startled.

He was quite happy in his new work, for we spent many an afternoon dozing in a cornfield not far from where his mother lived, and when the sun seemed hot enough to bake the whole crop into one gigantic loaf, it was no trouble to him to go over and fetch a bottle of iced orange-juice. In fact, he was very relieved to move from his old job as a roadsweeper, for a bitter feud had developed between his crew and the sweepers from the adjacent local authority, and bad feeling was foreign to his nature. The trouble brewed whenever they walked up the road leading out of town to find that a heap of dust — which was plainly the property of the District Council — had been deposited just inside the borough boundary. Naturally, they would at once push it back where it belonged, but within a few days it would be sitting on their side once again, and a little more besides. So, for weeks on end they would play out this game of dustman's ping-pong until a mountain of earth dominated the edge of the pavement, and householders could only watch with growing anxiety as it shuttled to and fro across the pavement in front of them. Then the winds would come and scatter the mound over all the neighbouring gardens and, a few days later, the process would begin all over again. The unpleasantness, more implied than expressed, played on his nerves and he was glad to be out of it; in any case, one of their sweepers was an ex-boxer.

As soon as Fingers joined us we were sent to clear away the wreckage of a public lavatory that had been demolished recently. The building had stood on the edge of Cundy Cross, and the story going around was that an extreme group of Women's Lib had wrecked it because its design rendered it suitable only for men. It was a messy job, for the lack of walls had not recently inhibited the more desperate travellers from making abundant and widespread use of it.

'Ah 'ope we're not doin' this all ' time,' said Fingers, screwing up his face.

'It's a pity Barney isn't with us,' I said, 'Because he's always wanted everything else before: he might have wanted to take this home with him.'

'Ah wonder if 'e does want it,' said Jake with a sly grin.

So we took it round to his home, and without anybody seeing us brought it piece by piece through the back garden gate. Finger's expression throughout was a mixture of puzzlement and concern, but apparently it bore no comparison to Barney's when he looked out of the window to find someone had erected a public urinal in the middle of his lawn.

A thunderous tattoo on the cabin roof woke us all with a start. It had been overcast all day, but such a cloudburst had come, as it were, out of the blue. Sleep was impossible with the roaring and whistling of the intense barrage, so we sat tight and peered at black shapes of shrubs and houses looming out of flickering, liquid sheets, while the streets and paths became turbulent rivers tumbling down the hillside and pitted by the fascinating, furious dance of the rain. For ten minutes or so the onslaught never let up, and then, as suddenly as it came, it petered out into a rather half-hearted drizzle, the trees were left to droop their bedraggled leaves and wrinkled streams raced down the gutters, bubbling over the choked drains.

But the storm had disturbed our rest, and with the rain almost stopped now, we decided to make one more trip before finishing for the day. We were parked on a small piece of waste ground at the bottom of a hill to which the only access was an earthen track running a concealed course behind a row of houses. The slope was steep, and the heavy downpour had turned the lane into oozing sludge, so that with the engine screaming and the wheels kicking in frantic desperation the wagon's progess was on a par with that of a yo-yo. After about ten attempts and still only half-way up, we felt the back wheels sinking once more deep into the ruts and the throbbing surge of the lorry subsided into an exhausted relapse. As we slid slowly back into the ditch we passed a man, looking most indignant, who was spattered from head to foot in thick, black mud.

'Why don't tha damn well look what tha're doin'?!' he yelled. 'What the 'Ell does tha think tha's got there, a bloody rabbit?'

It took so long to climb out of the hollow that, when we reached the junction with the road, the same man, in a complete change of clothes and his face brightly polished, was walking down the opposite pavement pushing a pram with a woman hanging on to his arm.

'Ah thought Ah recognized 'im,' said Jake at once. 'It's 'is wife what Randy Steve's been knockin' abaht wi'.'

We glanced again at this living portrait of domestic bliss.

'It looks like she's kept that quiet,' Fingers observed. 'Unless 'e's stickin' for t' sake o' ' bairn.'

'That's summat else she's kept quiet abaht an' all: that i'nt 'is kid. 'E's as sterile as a brass monkey, yon. 'E's been tryin' to get 'er i' ' family way for years, an' what wi' 'im bein' Catholic an' all, 'e were draggin' 'er off to church every Sunday to pray. Wuh, tha could tell bi just lookin' at 'er it weren't prayer she wanted. Any 'ow, since Steve put 'er i' ' club, there's nowt 'e won't do for 'er an' ' bairn; 'e lets 'er walk all o'er 'im — an' 'e's down at church every day now, 'cos 'e thinks 'e's 'ad a miracle.'

Our journey took us into one of the more expensive areas of Barnsley. An extremely attractive woman answered the doorbell, a face that I thought familiar, but she appeared so pleasant and genteel that I considered it wiser not to remind her that when we last met, she was revealing a few graphic home truths about Brian while he was lying across the bonnet of her car. She led us to the garage and politely asked if we would mind emptying it. There was very little, a dressing table and matching wardrobe, a roll of carpet and a few empty boxes. We could have loaded it up in under ten minutes, but as the woman walked back to the house, Fingers nudged Jake.

'Ah could do wi' this furniture for Joyce an' Linda,' he whispered.

Joyce emerged as the woman with whom he was living, and Linda was her child by the man she had divorced in order to marry her present husband. They were acquiring furniture as best they could, but apparently were still desperately short of dressing-tables, wardrobes and bedroom carpets. There was nothing to prevent us, short of a policeman, from dropping them off at his home that very afternoon, but there was already a ton of rubble on the back, and Fingers was understandably not keen to line his love-nest with fittings that had been battered for twenty minutes by a hail of half-bricks. At his suggestion we decided to pick them up later, so we told the woman that we had only room that day for the smaller items. What we did not go on to explain was that they included an enormous quantity of empty beer bottles, which were not, strictly speaking, in the garage, as they had been dumped behind it. We had a shrewd suspicion that they had been put there deliberately so that we should not see them, for the refund fetched nearly six pounds, but there was every reason to feel confident that in so affluent a district, an air of respectability was well worth the price of silence and a few hundred beer bottles.

When we arrived at the yard on the following morning, Fingers seemed quietly disturbed.

'Tha knows that bloke wi' all that furniture,' he neatly reminded us. ''E's a Labour councillor. Ah think it's disgustin'.'

'What's wrong with a Labour councillor having furniture?'

'Nowt. But look at ' posh 'ouse 'e lives in.'

'Yes, but you don't have to give up all your worldly goods to be a Socialist — unless you're the Son of God, of course.'

'Nay, what Ah mean is 'e says one thing an' does another. 'E didn't live in a 'ouse like that afore 'e got o' Council, tha knows. They all go on abaht 'ow they're workin' class lads aht to 'elp their own kind, but 'ow many when they've got into Parliament an' such like are content to live wi' ' workin' classes an' 'ave no more na what they've 'elped ' workin' classes to get? Ah mean, just look at this Labour Government. 'Ow many on 'em 'ave got in 'cos they're bahn to 'elp workin' people an' come away wi' two or three 'ouses? Who are they tryin' to 'elp, that's what Ah want to know? It's all reight them sayin' they're goin' to stop rich people gettin' fat by usin' poor folk. When they talk abaht rich people, they mean factory bosses an' ' like; but to us folk it means them in Parliament wi' two or three 'ouses.'

'Well, if your Labour councillor uses his position to look after himself, why keep re-electing him?'

''Cos everybody knows if tha put a donkey up as Labour

candidate i' Barnsley, it'd get elected. It's 'appened often enough i'
' past, any'ow.'

'I never realized before that you were a Tory, Fingers.'

'Ah weren't, till Ah saw everybody else were.'

'But what's the point of being a Tory dustman?'

'Why not? Take today, for instance. What Ah'm doin' today is
bein' a Tory. Ah'm bahn to nick as much aht o' that garage as Ah
can lay mi 'ands on.'

By some good fortune, the day proved remarkably ripe for
Fingers to advance his political principles. After we had collected
his half-bedroom suite and stored it temporarily behind the bushes
at the sewage farm, he obtained in the course of the morning four
chairs, a folding table, a double-bed and another wardrobe from a
house at Stairfoot, and a mangy-looking settee from a shop at
Pogmoor. As a finishing touch, the final call of the day provided
him with an upright piano. Warped by damp and its side riddled
with woodworm, it had lost a dozen of its keys, and the rest
sounded, as Jake put it, like a chorus of cracked bed-pans, but
Fingers saw this crumbling wreck as the most wonderful gift for his
darling Linda, and his eyes watered as he pictured her tiny fingers
flitting joyfully over the yellow ivory with intuitive skill. It was a
magnificent haul for one day, and Fingers was drunk with ecstasy:
the house at Stairfoot even threw in four regulation gas-masks
issued in the last war.

After a short afternoon nap, we took the collection round to
Finger's house. The back yard seemed to have been purpose-built
for the furtherance of furtive activities, dismal, poky and
surrounded on all sides by high, soot-stained walls. Fingers barred
the gates to screen us from the roadway, and then fetched Joyce out
from her kitchen so that she could watch the trophies he had
brought her being unloaded one by one. As they came off the
wagon she touched, examined and walked round them, tutting and
fretting and scolding him for bringing it all when they had not the
space and it only meant more work for her, but her bright eyes and
her quivering voice could not disguise that she was pleased as he
was, and as proud of a man as a woman could be. But her face did
fall when she saw the piano.

'What's that?!' she asked, sharply.

'A piana,' Fingers said, confidently. 'For Linda.'

'Well, it's not comin' in ' 'ouse. It can stop i' ' yard.'

'Nay, love. She can't play ahtside. She'll catch 'er death o' cold when it rains.'

'It's not comin' inside, any'ow an' that's final. What 'ave yer brought it 'er for?'

'To play.'

'But she can't play.'

'Course not, 'cos she's nivver 'ad a piana afore.'

The piano, however, remained in the yard. Joyce busied herself making tea while we dragged, bumped and swore the pieces inside and up the narrow staircase. There was not much room in the kitchen afterwards with several chairs, a table and a carpet clogging the existing arrangement, but Fingers said he would organize it when we had gone. The tea as it came out would have passed anywhere else as pea soup, and we drank it slowly; slowly, because it tasted strongly of paint, and you could only improve the flavour by a liberal dose of condensed milk from a tin or by hacking sugar out of the bag. I was lucky enough to have a mug with a long crack down the side, so that by sitting next to me on the draining board, it emptied itself in a way that might otherwise have seemed impolite.

"E's been back again today,' said Joyce. 'Ah thowt yer were goin' to speak to 'im.'

'Ah will, love. Ah will. It's just as Ah've 'ad other things to do … It's 'er 'usband's brother,' he obliged us.

'Ah was 'opin' yer'd get back an' 'ave it aht wi' 'im. 'E was 'ere at 'afe-past-nine.'

'Well, what did yer let 'im in for?'

'Ah didn't. Ah opened ' door an' 'e were there, an' afore Ah could shut it 'e put 'is foot i' ' way. 'E were stinkin' o' drink an' goin' on abaht 'e'd come in an' aht as 'e pleased an' what 'e'd do to mi if Ah tried to stop 'im. An' 'e's laid on that couch all day drinkin' an' sleepin' an' 'e's been sick o' ' floor, an' Ah've not been able to do nowt. Our Linda came 'ome early an' all so Ah 'ad to send 'er aht o' way to Mrs Roberts.'

'Don't worry, love. Leave it to me. Ah'll 'ave a word wi' 'im.'

'It 'i'nt as though 'e's a reight to be 'ere. Ah 'ad enough of 'im afore. All Ah want is to be left alone an' 'ave a nice 'ome.'

The rays of the afternoon sun poured through the window and tinged with gold her wan, hollow cheeks and the untidy wisps of hair beneath her scarf. The painted walls, cracked and blistered, glowed with warmth, lighting the brass plates on the mantelpiece and even the dusky skin of 'Tina' over the sideboard. From one end to the other there was a jumble of chairs, tables and rolls of carpets, a sea of woods and fibres in a cosy brown. The clock over the door ticked on happily, and if you looked hard at its face you could see the bloated reflection of the bright-green cupboards opposite and the mottled-enamel gas stove with the enormous egg-timer from Blackpool perched on top. A strange quietness fell upon the room. Jake coughed with embarrassment and he and I went out to put the piano back on to the wagon.

'It's a funny thing,' he said, 'But our lass's just t' same. Allus goin' on abaht 'avin' a nice 'ome. For me it's reight enough as it is. But they're nivver satisfied: allus wantin' that bit more.'

The piano was much too heavy for both of us to lift, and our attempts to lever it aboard using the tailboard ended dramatically when the side and front panels, together with several keys, disintegrated in a cloud of dust about our feet.

'Mind, Ah can understand 'er not wantin' this in 'er front room,' he continued. 'If they let ' little lass get on 'ere above 'afe an hour, she'd 'ave less fingers left than 'e 'as.'

Those days are gone, now, and long ago, but I remember them as though it all happened only yesterday. There was a strange magic in them, when even the most commonplace occasions seemed tinged with romance. They brought such freshness and vitality dancing in their train, a time of surging freedom and filled with the racy zest of youth. It was pleasure beyond telling then just to stand on the back of the spare wagon, gripping the headboard, while the lorry roared down the hill with the wind whistling ice-cold in your face and running its fingers through your streaming hair, to crouch over a canteen table with sixpennyworth of chips in one hand and a king-flush in the other, or to lie, devil-may-care, all morning in the quiet seclusion of a disused tip watching the naive busyness of nature or helpless with laughter at the pithy yarns of a round, red-faced dustman. These are the things best remembered, and somehow it is easy to forget the squalor, the sadness, the drudgery, the uncomfortable sense of degradation, and the soul-destroying hopelessness of the lowly man sweeping up his life down an endless road.

And still the bright suns grow brighter, and the terraced houses and quaint arcades are glazed with gold, while the breathless air lies warm and ever more drowsily over the spreading fields and the dusty hedges. Yet that is almost all that is left, a few lingering memories. Dustmen do not come down to the yard in Pontefract Road any more — the Cleansing Department removed to other premises some years ago — and the depot, now accommodating a wide variety of small trades, rings with different cries from the sounds of those memorable summers. The wooden canteen stands deserted and quiet; gaunt rafters reach out of the other buildings into the sky like enormous ribs where at one time there had been long, gray roofs of slate, and the once-hallowed office of the Superintendent is reduced to a dirty, pathetic-looking hovel.

But the past is not quite gone from the old depot. Even today you can see here and there a rusty shovel or a brush handle poking out of the weeds. The little red gate still bears the name of the Department in faded white lettering, like a faithful old servant unwilling to change his master. And sometimes, as I pass by in the early morning light when the mists are rising and the streets are silent, there seem to be in the shadows of the derelict sheds the dim shapes of men in donkey jackets and blue overalls lounging against handcarts, and lorries are raising the dust in a circling convoy round the yard, the inspector's office is a hive of commotion, and above all the noise and babble comes the shrill echo of the little clocking-on bell.

The last time I saw Jake was nearly a year later. I was on a bus travelling towards Penistone, about seven miles from Barnsley, when, just a little way from the town, I saw a lorry of seemingly familiar proportions half-hidden on some waste ground. At first sight it appeared silly even to suppose that a vehicle belonging to Barnsley Corporation would have wandered so far from home, but as we came closer there could no longer be any doubt that it was the spare wagon. It was difficult to see inside the cabin, for the sun was reflecting strongly from the windscreen, but the side window was open, and there was the unmistakeable shape of its driver slouched in his seat, his mouth gaping wide and a tangle of thinning red hair resting on a small head-cushion. He was asleep.